Linux

System Administration & Practical Management Guidelines

Nathan Clark

© **Copyright 2019 Nathan Clark.**
All rights reserved.

No part of this publication may be reproduced, distributed, or transmitted in any form or by any means, including photocopying, recording, or other electronic or mechanical methods, without the prior written permission of the publisher, except in the case of brief quotations embodied in critical reviews and certain other noncommercial uses permitted by copyright law.

Every effort has been made to ensure that the content provided herein is accurate and helpful for our readers at publishing time. However, this is not an exhaustive treatment of the subjects. No liability is assumed for losses or damages due to the information provided.

Any trademarks which are used are done so without consent and any use of the same does not imply consent or permission was gained from the owner. Any trademarks or brands found within are purely used for clarification purposes and no owners are in any way affiliated with this work.

Books in this Series

LINUX

Installation, Configuration and Command Line Basics

LINUX

System Administration &
Practical Management Guidelines

Table of Contents

About This Book 1

1. The Linux Boot Process 3
    1.1 Alternative Boot Loaders 8
    1.2 Reviewing the Boot Process 10
    1.3 Commands to Restart and Stop the System 12

2. Hardware Management 15
    2.1 Using the /proc Filesystem 15
    2.2 Command Line Tools 19
    2.3 Graphical Tools 21

3. Shared Libraries 23
    3.1 Naming Conventions 24
    3.2 Identifying Referenced Libraries using ldd 25
    3.3 Identifying Referenced Libraries using objdump 26

4. User and Group Management 29
    4.1 User and Group Commands 34

5. Filesystems 43
    5.1 Types of Commonly Used Filesystems 45
    5.2 Filesystem Commands 49
    5.3 Practical Example 50

6. Disk Storage Management 53
    6.1 Naming the Devices 53
    6.2 Primary, Extended, and Logical Partitions 54
    6.3 udev and df 57
    6.4 Mounting a Filesystem 60
    6.5 Unmounting a Filesystem 61
    6.6 Automating Mount Points 62
    6.7 Setting up New Partitions 65

7. Working with Links 77
7.1 Hard Links 77
7.2 Soft Links 79
7.3 Practical Example 80
8. Text Processing 83
8.1 Text Processing Commands 83
8.2 Combining Commands 94
9. Package Management 97
9.1 Understanding Package Architecture 97
9.2 Day-to-Day Administration Tasks 102
10. Log Files 107
10.1 Important Log Files 107
10.2 Essential Commands & Graphical Tools 111
11. Process Management 115
11.1 Working with Processes 115
12. System and Network Security 125
12.1 Open Ports 125
12.2 Local and Remote Users 128
12.3 Restricting Remote Access 132
12.4 Unused Software 133
Further Reading 135
About the Author 137

About This Book

This guide is the second book in our three-part Linux series. In the chapters that follow we look at the administration and management tasks required to keep a Linux system running. It includes network security, user and group management, working with libraries, hardware and software management, filesystems and storage, interpreting log files, and other aspects every proficient Linux user should know.

To get the most value out of this guide, it is recommended to have a basic knowledge of Linux and its general usage. If you are unfamiliar with the basics of a Linux system, or just a little rusty, we suggest first reading through our comprehensive beginner's guide. **Linux: Installation, Configuration and Command Line Basics.** There we show you how to set up and configure a Linux system, how the command line works, and much more.

For the examples in this book, we use the Debian GNU/Linux distribution as a reference point. However the majority of the explanations apply to most distributions, and Debian is merely what we use and prefer due to its outstanding stability. You are more than welcome to use a different Linux distribution.

1. The Linux Boot Process

We start off by looking at the first process in all Linux systems, the boot process. Starting up a UNIX/Linux system is a complex multi-part process, which consists of the following high-level steps:

1. The Basic Input Output System (BIOS) executes the Master Boot Record (MBR). Newer systems use the Unified Extensible Firmware Interface (UEFI).

2. The MBR executes a boot loader, such as the Grand Unified Bootloader (GRUB) or the Linux Loader (LILO).

3. The boot loader then executes the Linux kernel.

4. The Linux kernel runs the *init* process via /sbin/init to start the operating system.

5. *Init* then executes *init.d* with *runlevels* or *systemd*.

These steps are explained in more detail below.

BIOS and UEFI

Either the BIOS or the UEFI is run when starting the computer. This software is delivered from a vendor-specific firmware memory chip on the computer's motherboard, specific to that motherboard. The BIOS or UEFI first performs some system integrity checks. Then it searches the hard drives, CD/DVD drives, USB drives and the network in a preselected order and boots the first boot loader program it finds. This boot loader is then loaded into memory and takes control of the system. In simple terms, the BIOS or UEFI loads, and executes the boot loader.

At startup there is usually an option to press F1, F2, F12, Escape or Delete to enter the BIOS or UEFI menu. The boot loader search sequence can be changed from here. Once changes are made, usually the F10 key saves the changes and restarts the system with the new settings. With most modern systems, BIOS is no longer used and has been replaced by UEFI BIOS. UEFI BIOS is maintained by the Unified EFI Forum. Support for UEFI by Debian is part of the default setup.

Compared to BIOS, the UEFI has the following advantages:

- The ability to use large-capacity disks (over 2 Terabytes) with a GUID Partition Table (GPT).
- CPU-independent architecture.
- CPU-independent drivers.
- A flexible pre-OS environment that includes network capability.
- A modular design.
- Backward and forward compatibility.

To determine if a Debian system is booted via UEFI, check for the directory /sys/firmware/efi. If that directory exists, the system is running in UEFI mode. A system without UEFI will return the following:

```
$ ls /sys/firmware/efi
ls: cannot access /sys/firmware/efi: No such file or directory
$
```

MBR

The Master Boot Record (MBR) is located in the first sector of the bootable disk. Typically, this is either /dev/hda or /dev/sda. It contains all information about the logical partitions on the disk. The MBR is less than 512 bytes in size and has the following three components:

1. Primary boot loader info in the first 446 bytes.

2. Partition table info in the next 64 bytes.

3. MBR validation check (signature) in the last two bytes.

The MBR contains information about GRUB. So in simple terms, it loads and executes the GRUB boot loader. The contents of the MBR may be viewed by combining the two commands *dd* (disk dump) and *hexdump* from the "coreutils" package and "bsdmainutils" package in the following manner:

```
# dd if=/dev/sda bs=512 count=1 | hexdump -C
```

In the above code *dd* reads the contents of the first SCSI disk /dev/sda, block by block as chunks of 512 bytes. The option *count=1* limits this step to reading the first block only. Then the output of *dd* is piped to *hexdump* using the option -C. The output of *hexdump* is shown as ASCII characters. The image below illustrates this in more detail.

```
user@debian95: ~
File  Edit  View  Search  Terminal  Help
root@debian95:/home/user# dd if=/dev/sda bs=512 count=1 | hexdump -C
00000000  eb 63 90 10 8e d0 bc 00  b0 b8 00 00 8e d8 8e c0  |.c..............|
00000010  fb be 00 7c bf 00 06 b9  00 02 f3 a4 ea 21 06 00  |...|.........!..|
00000020  00 be be 07 38 04 75 0b  83 c6 10 81 fe fe 07 75  |....8.u........u|
00000030  f3 eb 16 b4 02 b0 01 bb  00 7c b2 80 8a 74 01 8b  |.........|...t..|
00000040  4c 02 cd 13 ea 00 7c 00  00 eb fe 00 00 00 00 00  |L.....|.........|
00000050  00 00 00 00 00 00 00 00  00 00 00 80 01 00 00 00  |................|
00000060  00 00 00 00 ff fa 90 90  f6 c2 80 74 05 f6 c2 70  |...........t...p|
00000070  74 02 b2 80 ea 79 7c 00  00 31 c0 8e d8 8e d0 bc  |t....y|..1......|
00000080  00 20 fb a0 64 7c 3c ff  74 02 88 c2 52 bb 17 04  |. ..d|<.t...R...|
00000090  f6 07 03 74 06 be 88 7d  e8 17 01 be 05 7c b4 41  |...t...}.....|.A|
000000a0  bb aa 55 cd 13 5a 52 72  3d 81 fb 55 aa 75 37 83  |..U..ZRr=..U.u7.|
000000b0  e1 01 74 32 31 c0 89 44  04 40 88 44 ff 89 44 02  |..t21..D.@.D..D.|
000000c0  c7 04 10 00 66 8b 1e 5c  7c 66 89 5c 08 66 8b 1e  |....f..\|f.\.f..|
000000d0  60 7c 66 89 5c 0c c7 44  06 00 70 b4 42 cd 13 72  |`|f.\..D..p.B..r|
000000e0  05 bb 00 70 eb 76 b4 08  cd 13 73 0d 5a 84 d2 0f  |...p.v....s.Z...|
000000f0  83 d0 00 be 93 7d e9 82  00 66 0f b6 c6 88 64 ff  |.....}...f....d.|
00000100  40 66 89 44 04 0f b6 d1  c1 e2 02 88 e8 88 f4 40  |@f.D...........@|
00000110  89 44 08 0f b6 c2 c0 e8  02 66 89 04 66 a1 60 7c  |.D.......f..f.`||
00000120  66 09 c0 75 4e 66 a1 5c  7c 66 31 d2 66 f7 34 88  |f..uNf.\|f1.f.4.|
00000130  d1 31 d2 66 f7 74 04 3b  44 08 7d 37 fe c1 88 c5  |.1.f.t.;D.}7....|
00000140  30 c0 c1 e8 02 08 c1 88  d0 5a 88 c6 bb 00 70 8e  |0........Z....p.|
00000150  c3 31 db b8 01 02 cd 13  72 1e 8c c3 60 1e b9 00  |.1......r...`...|
00000160  01 8e db 31 f6 bf 00 80  8e c6 fc f3 a5 1f 61 ff  |...1..........a.|
00000170  26 5a 7c be 8e 7d eb 03  be 9d 7d e8 34 00 be a2  |&Z|..}....}.4...|
00000180  7d e8 2e 00 cd 18 eb fe  47 52 55 42 20 00 47 65  |}.......GRUB .Ge|
00000190  6f 6d 00 48 61 72 64 20  44 69 73 6b 00 52 65 61  |om.Hard Disk.Rea|
000001a0  64 00 20 45 72 72 6f 72  0d 0a 00 bb 01 00 b4 0e  |d. Error........|
000001b0  cd 10 ac 3c 00 75 f4 c3  27 82 24 1c 00 00 80 20  |...<.u..'.$.... |
000001c0  21 00 83 05 56 6f 00 08  00 00 00 f0 59 00 00 25  |!...Vo......Y..%|
000001d0  75 6f 05 fe ff ff fe ff  59 00 02 f8 85 01 00 00  |uo......Y.......|
000001e0  00 00 00 00 00 00 00 00  00 00 00 00 00 00 00 00  |................|
000001f0  00 00 00 00 00 00 00 00  00 00 00 00 00 00 55 aa  |..............U.|
```

The *dd* command can also be used to create a backup of the MBR as shown below. The output file is "mbr.bin" and is specified using the option *of=mbr.bin*, where *of* abbreviates from "output file".

```
# dd if=/dev/sda bs=512 count=1 of=mbr.bin
```

```
user@debian95: ~
File  Edit  View  Search  Terminal  Help
root@debian95:/home/user# dd if=/dev/sda bs=512 count=1 of=mbr.bin
1+0 records in
1+0 records out
512 bytes copied, 0.000371249 s, 1.4 MB/s
root@debian95:/home/user# file mbr.bin
mbr.bin: DOS/MBR boot sector
root@debian95:/home/user#
```

GRUB

The software that handles the Linux startup is called the Grand Unified Bootloader (GRUB), or GNU GRUB to be precise. Its function is to take over from the BIOS at boot time, load itself, load the Linux kernel into memory, and then turn over execution to the Linux kernel. Once the kernel takes over, GRUB has done its job and is no longer needed.

Note that GRUB version 1 has been replaced by GRUB2, the former is now referred to as GRUB Legacy. For simplicity, GRUB2 is simply called GRUB.

At boot time, GRUB displays a splash screen and presents a menu from which to start the system. The more Linux kernel images present on the system, the longer the list of entries. The image below shows the default installation with two menu entries. Unless otherwise stated, the first menu points to the default entry.

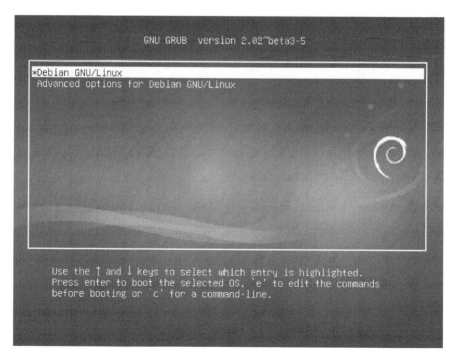

GRUB waits for a few seconds, then loads the kernel image selected from the menu. The first entry targets the default image specified in the GRUB configuration file /boot/grub2/grub.cfg. This configuration file is first generated during Linux installation and automatically regenerated whenever a new Linux kernel is installed.

Linux Kernel

In this step, the root filesystem is mounted as specified in the entry "root=" in the GRUB configuration file. Then the kernel executes the /sbin/init program. The kernel uses a file called "initrd", short for Initial RAM Disk, as a temporary root filesystem until the kernel is booted and the real root filesystem is mounted. It contains all necessary drivers to access hard drive partitions, filesystems, and other hardware components.

1.1 Alternative Boot Loaders

GRUB is not the only boot loader in the open-source world. Other boot loaders include:

BURG
　　The name abbreviates to Brand-new Unified loadeR from GRUB (a bit of a stretch to get the reverse of GRUB if you ask us). It is an offshoot of GRUB with much more room for individual configuration.

SYSLINUX
　　A lightweight boot loader for networks and CD/DVD drives.

ISOLINUX
　　A boot loader from the SYSLINUX project, which is

generally used for Linux Live CDs and bootable install CDs.

gummiboot

A boot loader for EFI-based computers with a text-mode interface. It is intended to be a minimal alternative to GNU GRUB that automatically detects bootable images (including Linux kernel images, operating systems, and other boot loaders), does not require a configuration file, provides a basic menu-based interface, and can also integrate with "systemd" to provide performance data.

Libreboot

A lightweight system designed to perform only the minimum number of tasks necessary to load and run a modern 32-bit or 64-bit operating system. The image below shows the menu for Libreboot.

rEFInd

A boot manager for EFI-based computers that features a GUI. rEFInd can be used to boot multiple operating systems, and it also provides a way to enter and explore the EFI pre-boot environment.

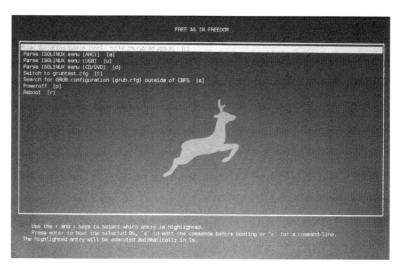

1.2 Reviewing the Boot Process

Linux generates a log file to enable review of the boot process and to read its accompanying messages. Before Linux 8, the boot log was stored as a text file in /var/log/boot. Linux 8 introduced "systemd" and the format and location changed. To retrieve the boot log, use *journalctl* as follows (must be root):

```
# journalctl -b
```

"Systemd" stores log messages in a special format. *journalctl* reads the log and displays messages in chronological order. The earliest entry comes first, and the entries can be scrolled back and forth using the arrow keys. The output consists of four columns: date (timestamp), hostname, message type kernel, and the message itself.

```
user@debian95: ~
File Edit View Search Terminal Help
-- Logs begin at Mon 2018-08-20 09:36:08 EDT, end at Tue 2018-09-04 19:09:58 EDT.
Aug 20 09:36:08 debian95 kernel: Linux version 4.9.0-7-amd64 (debian-kernel@lists.
Aug 20 09:36:08 debian95 kernel: Command line: BOOT_IMAGE=/boot/vmlinuz-4.9.0-7-am
Aug 20 09:36:08 debian95 kernel: x86/fpu: Legacy x87 FPU detected.
Aug 20 09:36:08 debian95 kernel: e820: BIOS-provided physical RAM map:
Aug 20 09:36:08 debian95 kernel: BIOS-e820: [mem 0x0000000000000000-0x0000000000009
Aug 20 09:36:08 debian95 kernel: BIOS-e820: [mem 0x000000000009fc00-0x0000000000009
Aug 20 09:36:08 debian95 kernel: BIOS-e820: [mem 0x00000000000f0000-0x00000000000f
Aug 20 09:36:08 debian95 kernel: BIOS-e820: [mem 0x0000000000100000-0x00000000c4ae
Aug 20 09:36:08 debian95 kernel: BIOS-e820: [mem 0x00000000c4af0000-0x00000000c4af
Aug 20 09:36:08 debian95 kernel: BIOS-e820: [mem 0x00000000fffc0000-0x00000000ffff
Aug 20 09:36:08 debian95 kernel: NX (Execute Disable) protection: active
Aug 20 09:36:08 debian95 kernel: SMBIOS 2.5 present.
Aug 20 09:36:08 debian95 kernel: DMI: innotek GmbH VirtualBox/VirtualBox, BIOS Vir
Aug 20 09:36:08 debian95 kernel: e820: update [mem 0x00000000-0x00000fff] usable =
Aug 20 09:36:08 debian95 kernel: e820: remove [mem 0x000a0000-0x000fffff] usable
Aug 20 09:36:08 debian95 kernel: e820: last_pfn = 0xc4af0 max_arch_pfn = 0x4000000
Aug 20 09:36:08 debian95 kernel: MTRR default type: uncachable
Aug 20 09:36:08 debian95 kernel: MTRR variable ranges disabled:
Aug 20 09:36:08 debian95 kernel: MTRR: Disabled
Aug 20 09:36:08 debian95 kernel: x86/PAT: MTRRs disabled, skipping PAT initializat
Aug 20 09:36:08 debian95 kernel: CPU MTRRs all blank - virtualized system.
Aug 20 09:36:08 debian95 kernel: x86/PAT: Configuration [0-7]: WB  WT  UC- UC  WB
Aug 20 09:36:08 debian95 kernel: found SMP MP-table at [mem 0x0009fff0-0x0009ffff]
Aug 20 09:36:08 debian95 kernel: Base memory trampoline at [ffff886440099000] 9900
Aug 20 09:36:08 debian95 kernel: BRK [0x8973a000, 0x8973afff] PGTABLE
Aug 20 09:36:08 debian95 kernel: BRK [0x8973b000, 0x8973bfff] PGTABLE
Aug 20 09:36:08 debian95 kernel: BRK [0x8973c000, 0x8973cfff] PGTABLE
Aug 20 09:36:08 debian95 kernel: BRK [0x8973d000, 0x8973dfff] PGTABLE
Aug 20 09:36:08 debian95 kernel: BRK [0x8973e000, 0x8973efff] PGTABLE
lines 1-30
```

In order to see the list of recorded boots, the *list-boots* option can be used. The output consists of three columns: the boot entry number (0 for the last entry), a hash to identify the entry, and a timestamp. The image below shows the output.

```
# journalctl --list-boots
```

```
user@debian95: ~/Desktop
File  Edit  View  Search  Terminal  Help
root@debian95:~# journalctl --list-boots
 0 5f41f5e968b34d068320f0f13237b7e2 Tue 2018-09-04 19:16:12 EDT—Wed 2018-09-05 1
lines 1-1/1 (END)
```

An alternative to *journalctl* is *dmesg*. This command allows you to see the entire boot process, including BIOS messages. The image below displays the output you would get. Each line consists of three parts: the date (timestamp) printed on the left in brackets, the component printed second and prior to the colon (:), and the message printed last. On a color monitor, these three parts are distinguished by color i.e. green, yellow and black.

```
user@debian95: ~/Desktop
File  Edit  View  Search  Terminal  Help
root@debian95:~#
root@debian95:~# dmesg
[    0.000000] Linux version 4.9.0-7-amd64 (debian-kernel@lists.debian.org) (gcc
 version 6.3.0 20170516 (Debian 6.3.0-18+deb9u1) ) #1 SMP Debian 4.9.110-1 (2018
-07-05)
[    0.000000] Command line: BOOT_IMAGE=/boot/vmlinuz-4.9.0-7-amd64 root=UUID=1d
4acbbf-4420-4eab-984d-ceebc408a51e ro quiet
[    0.000000] x86/fpu: Legacy x87 FPU detected.
[    0.000000] e820: BIOS-provided physical RAM map:
[    0.000000] BIOS-e820: [mem 0x0000000000000000-0x000000000009fbff] usable
[    0.000000] BIOS-e820: [mem 0x000000000009fc00-0x000000000009ffff] reserved
[    0.000000] BIOS-e820: [mem 0x00000000000f0000-0x00000000000fffff] reserved
[    0.000000] BIOS-e820: [mem 0x0000000000100000-0x00000000c4aeffff] usable
[    0.000000] BIOS-e820: [mem 0x00000000c4af0000-0x00000000c4afffff] ACPI data
[    0.000000] BIOS-e820: [mem 0x00000000fffc0000-0x00000000ffffffff] reserved
[    0.000000] NX (Execute Disable) protection: active
[    0.000000] SMBIOS 2.5 present.
[    0.000000] DMI: innotek GmbH VirtualBox/VirtualBox, BIOS VirtualBox 12/01/20
06
[    0.000000] e820: update [mem 0x00000000-0x00000fff] usable ==> reserved
[    0.000000] e820: remove [mem 0x000a0000-0x000fffff] usable
[    0.000000] e820: last_pfn = 0xc4af0 max_arch_pfn = 0x400000000
[    0.000000] MTRR default type: uncachable
[    0.000000] MTRR variable ranges disabled:
[    0.000000] MTRR: Disabled
[    0.000000] x86/PAT: MTRRs disabled, skipping PAT initialization too.
[    0.000000] CPU MTRRs all blank - virtualized system.
[    0.000000] x86/PAT: Configuration [0-7]: WB  WT  UC- UC  WB  WT  UC- UC
[    0.000000] found SMP MP-table at [mem 0x000fffa0-0x000fffff] mapped at [ffff
```

11

1.3 Commands to Restart and Stop the System

There are a number of common commands available when it comes to restarting and stopping the system. To reboot Linux, you can use either *reboot* or *shutdown*. To stop Linux, you can invoke *halt, poweroff* or *shutdown*. Below we will discuss a number of practical examples.

```
# shutdown -r now
```

The above command will restart the system. The option *-r* designates a reboot and restarts the system. The option *now* is a time parameter and invokes the action immediately. You can also use the *reboot* command to perform the exact same action as the *shutdown -r now* command.

```
# reboot
```

The *shutdown* command can also be used to stop the system by using the *-h* option instead. This instructs Linux to halt.

```
# shutdown -h now
```

Again, the *now* time parameter is used to stop the system immediately. The time parameter can also be specified as an exact time. The command shown in the image below will shut down the system after five minutes. It will also inform all users about the shutdown by sending them a relevant message. The message will be visible on all open terminals.

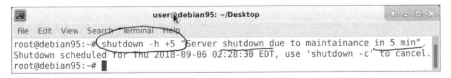

Similar to rebooting the system, stopping Linux also has a shortcut in the form of the _halt_ command. This performs the same action as the _shutdown -h now_ command.

```
# halt
```

The _halt_, _poweroff_ and _reboot_ commands stop the system immediately. They are similar to _shutdown -h now_ except that the _shutdown_ command terminates all processes gracefully, instead of killing them abruptly. Keep in mind that all the commands above require administrative privileges to be executed. They cannot be executed by a regular user.

* use "shutdown" command versus "halt", "poweroff", "reboot". the former ends Linux properly, whereas the latter commands abruptly "kill" the processes.

2. Hardware Management

Automatic hardware detection used to be somewhat of a gamble, as hardware wasn't always detected automatically all of the time. It used to be necessary to probe the hardware to figure out what was installed. In the last few years, this has improved significantly as manufacturers document their products in more detail and publish the specs online. This has led to an extended knowledge database and support.

2.1 Using the /proc Filesystem

/proc is a virtual filesystem, also referred to as an in-memory filesystem, created by the Linux kernel at runtime. It displays information about the kernel, processes, and other system information. This information is displayed in a file structure and accessible to everyone. As an example, the image below shows the contents of /proc/cmdline, which are the options the Linux kernel was invoked with.

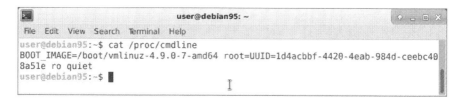

Some other useful files are:

/proc/cpuinfo
Information about the computer's CPU.

/proc/meminfo
Information about system memory.

/proc/loadvg
Load average. The first three columns measure CPU utilization from the last 1, 5 and 10 minutes. The fourth column shows the number of currently running processes and the total number of processes. The last column displays the last process ID used.

/proc/partitions
Partition-related information.

/proc/version
Information about the Linux version.

```
$ cat /proc/version
Linux version 3.16.0-4-amd64 (debian-
kernel@lists.debian.org) (gcc version 4.8.4 (Debian 4.8.4-1) )
#1 SMP Debian 3.16.43-2+deb8u2 (2017-06-26)
$
```

/proc/devices
List of device drivers configured into the currently running kernel.

/proc/filesystems
Lists the filesystems supported by the kernel.

/proc/uptime
Contains information about the running time of the system. The first number is the total number of seconds

the system has been up. The second number is how much of that time the machine has spent idle, in seconds.

```
$ cat /proc/uptime
15250.54 55603.02
$
```

Processes in Linux are assigned a number of files. The image below shows the file structure for the process with the process ID (PID) of 433. Following this, we look at the purpose and contents of the files generally available.

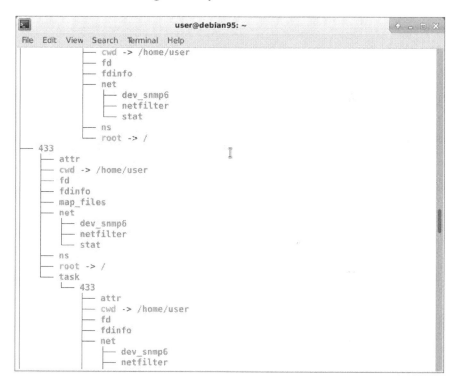

/proc/PID/cmdline
Command line arguments.

/proc/PID/cpu
Current and last CPU in which the process was executed.

/proc/PID/cwd
   Link to the current working directory.

/proc/PID/environ
   Values of the environment variables.

/proc/PID/exe
   Link to the executable of this process.

/proc/PID/fd
   Directory that contains all file descriptors.

/proc/PID/maps
   Maps to executables and library files.

/proc/PID/mem
   Memory held by this process.

/proc/PID/root
   Link to the root directory of this process.

/proc/PID/stat
   Status of the process.

/proc/PID/statm
   Process memory status information.

/proc/PID/status
   Process status in human readable form.

If you want to learn more about the /proc filesystem, check out the manpage for /proc. It covers much more than what is relevant for the scope of this guide.

2.2 Command Line Tools

Detect the CPU Using cpuid

In order to get more information about the CPU in your Linux system, use the *cpuid* command. This tool is available from the Debian package "cpuid". An example of the detailed information returned by this command is shown below.

```
$ cpuid
CPU 0:
vendor_id = "GenuineIntel"
version information (1/eax):
        processor type   = primary processor (0)
        family    = Intel Pentium Pro/II/III/Celeron/Core/Core
        2/Atom, AMD Athlon/Duron-, Cyrix M2, VIA C3 (6)
        model              = 0xd (13)
        stepping id        = 0x4 (4)
        extended family   = 0x0 (0)
        extended model    = 0x3 (3)
        (simple synth)     = Intel Pentium II / Pentium III /
        Pentium M / Celeron / Celcron M /-Core / Core 2 / Core i
        / Xeon / Atom (unknown model)
miscellaneous (1/ebx):
        process local APIC physical ID        = 0x0 (0)
        cpu count                              = 0x10 (16)
        CLFLUSH line size                      = 0x8 (8)
        brand index                            = 0x0 (0)
brand id = 0x00 (0): unknown
feature information (1/edx):
        x87 FPU on chip                        = true
        virtual-8086 mode enhancement          = true
        debugging extensions                   = true
        page size extensions                   = true
        time stamp counter                     = true
        RDMSR and WRMSR support                = true
        physical address extensions            = true
```

```
            machine check exception          = true
            CMPXCHG8B inst.                  = true
            APIC on chip                     = true
    ...
$
```

Detect Hardware Using dmidecode

The tool "dmidecode" reports detailed data about installed system components such as the processor, motherboard and RAM. This information is based on the Desktop Management Interface (DMI), a framework that classifies the individual components of a desktop, notebook or server by abstracting them from the software that manages them. This tool is available via the Debian package of the same name. The image below shows the output when executed in Debian via a VirtualBox environment.

```
                            user@debian95: ~                    _ □ x
File  Edit  View  Search  Terminal  Help
root@debian95:/home/user# dmidecode
# dmidecode 3.0
Getting SMBIOS data from sysfs.
SMBIOS 2.5 present.
10 structures occupying 450 bytes.
Table at 0x000E1000.

Handle 0x0000, DMI type 0, 20 bytes
BIOS Information
        Vendor: innotek GmbH
        Version: VirtualBox
        Release Date: 12/01/2006
        Address: 0xE0000
        Runtime Size: 128 kB
        ROM Size: 128 kB
        Characteristics:
                ISA is supported
                PCI is supported
                Boot from CD is supported
                Selectable boot is supported
                8042 keyboard services are supported (int 9h)
                CGA/mono video services are supported (int 10h)
                ACPI is supported

Handle 0x0001, DMI type 1, 27 bytes
System Information
        Manufacturer: innotek GmbH
        Product Name: VirtualBox
        Version: 1.2
        Serial Number: 0
```

2.3 Graphical Tools

Graphical tools are also available that are able to collect and display hardware information. These tools provide a graphical user interface, which many users prefer. Some of these tools include Hardware Lister (lshw-gtk) and "hardinfo". The image below presents memory information using "hardinfo".

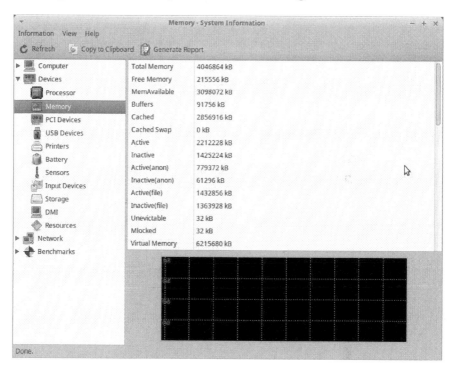

3. Shared Libraries

Linux, like any operating system, contains collections of files used for different purposes such as binary files (compiled program code), runtime interpreted code (written in programs like Perl or Python), configuration files, log files, libraries, and user data.

In the world of programming, a library is an assortment of pre-compiled pieces of code that can be used in other programs. These libraries contain functions, classes and data structures. They allow the reuse of code that already exists and has already been tested, so the user doesn't need to reinvent the wheel. As a result, libraries simplify life for programmers significantly. Among the most prominent examples of libraries in Linux are "libc", the standard C library, and "glibc", the GNU version of "libc".

Linux distinguishes between statically and dynamically linked binary programs. Statically linked, means the routines from the library become part of the program. In contrast, dynamically linked means the routines from the library are referenced only and do not become part of the program. Statically linked programs are entirely independent of one another but require more disk space. Dynamically linked programs are smaller but depend on the reference libraries, meaning they load quicker if the referenced library is already in memory. These libraries are called shared libraries or dynamic libraries.

3.1 Naming Conventions

It is common to extend the filename of a shared library with ".so" which abbreviates the term "shared object". Apart from the filename, a shared library also has a library name known as a "soname".

As an example, the soname for "libc" is "libc.so.6". Here "lib" is the prefix, "c" is a descriptive name, "so" is short for "shared object", and "6" is the version of the library (the version of the Application Binary Interface or ABI). The filename including the path is /lib64/ libc.so.6. Note that the soname is actually a symbolic link to the filename. Usually these files reside in the following directories:

default paths
/usr/local/lib, /usr/local/lib64, /usr/lib, /usr/lib64

system startup libraries
/lib, /lib64

Programmers can however install libraries in custom locations. The library path is defined in the configuration file /etc/ld.so.conf. Defining the library location can be done in the following manner:

```
$ cat /etc/ld.so.conf
include /etc/ld.so.conf.d/*.conf
$
```

The following command illustrates how to find the shared libraries on your Linux system using the *find* command:

```
$ find / -name *.so
/lib/klibc-IpHGKKbZiB_yZ7GPagmQz2GwVAQ.so
/lib/security/pam_vbox.so
/lib/security/pam_gnome_keyring.so
/lib/x86_64-linux-gnu/libnss_hesiod-2.19.so
/lib/x86_64-linux-gnu/libnss_compat-2.19.so
/lib/x86_64-linux-gnu/libnss_files-2.19.so
/lib/x86_64-linux-gnu/libnss_dns-2.19.so
/lib/x86_64-linux-gnu/security/pam_namespace.so
/lib/x86_64-linux-gnu/security/pam_env.so
/lib/x86_64-linux-gnu/security/pam_filter.so
...
$
```

3.2 Identifying Referenced Libraries using ldd

To find out which shared objects a binary file uses, we can use the command *ldd*. For example, to find the shared objects of the file manager Midnight Commander (mc), type *ldd /usr/bin/mc*. Each line within the output consists of the soname followed by the filename and the hash value in brackets.

```
$ ldd /usr/bin/mc
         linux-vdso.so.1 (0x00007ffd555fb000)
         libslang.so.2 => /lib/x86_64-linux-gnu/libslang.so.2
         (0x00007f483d6bb000)
         libgpm.so.2 => /usr/lib/x86_64-linux-gnu/libgpm.so.2
         (0x00007f483d4b5000)
         libext2fs.so.2 => /lib/x86_64-linux-gnu/libext2fs.so.2
         (0x00007f483d26e000)
         libssh2.so.1 => /usr/lib/x86_64-linux-gnu/libssh2.so.1
         (0x00007f483d045000)
         libgmodule-2.0.so.0 => /usr/lib/x86_64-linux-
         gnu/libgmodule-2.0.so.0 (0 -x00007f483ce41000)
```

```
        libglib-2.0.so.0 => /lib/x86_64-linux-gnu/libglib-2.0.so.0
        (0x00007f483cb31000)
        libpthread.so.0 => /lib/x86_64-linux-gnu/libpthread.so.0
        (0x00007f483c914000)
        libc.so.6 => /lib/x86_64-linux-gnu/libc.so.6
        (0x00007f483c569000)
        libdl.so.2 => /lib/x86_64-linux-gnu/libdl.so.2
        (0x00007f483c364000)
        libm.so.6 => /lib/x86_64-linux-gnu/libm.so.6
        (0x00007f483c063000)
        libcom_err.so.2 => /lib/x86_64-linux-
        gnu/libcom_err.so.2 (0x00007f483be5f000)
        libz.so.1 => /lib/x86_64-linux-gnu/libz.so.1
        (0x00007f483bc43000)
        libgcrypt.so.20 => /lib/x86_64-linux-gnu/libgcrypt.so.20
        (0x00007f483b962000)
        libpcre.so.3 => /lib/x86_64-linux-gnu/libpcre.so.3
        (0x00007f483b6f4000)
        /lib64/ld-linux-x86-64.so.2 (0x0000555cbfa60000)
        libgpg-error.so.0 => /lib/x86_64-linux-gnu/libgpg-
        error.so.0 (0x00007f483b4e1000)
$
```

If the binary file is a statically linked program the output of *ldd* is as follows:

```
$ ldd /usr/bin/ldd
not a dynamic executable
$
```

3.3 Identifying Referenced Libraries using objdump

An alternative to *ldd* is *objdump*. The following example combines *objdump* and *grep* in order to filter only the lines that contain the required shared objects.

The program "mc" requires the eight shared libraries seen below.

```
$ objdump -p /usr/bin/mc | grep NEEDED
NEEDED      libslang.so.2
NEEDED      libgpm.so.2
NEEDED      libext2fs.so.2
NEEDED      libssh2.so.1
NEEDED      libgmodule-2.0.so.0
NEEDED      libglib-2.0.so.0
NEEDED      libpthread.so.0
NEEDED      libc.so.6
$
```

4. User and Group Management

Linux is a multi-user operating system, which means multiple users can have access to the Linux system at the same time. In order for the system to manage these different users and groups, it stores this data in a number of configuration files:

/etc/passwd
>   user data (see Section 4.2)

/etc/shadow
>   encrypted user passwords (see Section 4.3)

/etc/group
>   group data (see Section 4.4)

/etc/gshadow
>   encrypted group passwords (see Section 4.5)

These files are text-based databases and have a defined structure. Below we will look at each of them in more detail. The contents of these files can be changed using a text editor, or with the commands *passwd*, *chage*, *chfn*, *chsh* and *usermod*.

/etc/passwd

This file contains all user attributes except the password. Each line consists of seven columns, and the columns are separated by a colon (:). The attributes are the username, the password, the user ID, the group ID, the GECOS field, the user's home directory, and the user's login shell.

The first attribute **username** refers to the UNIX username, and it must be unique to the system. The **password** field only contains an x. The value of the password has moved to /etc/shadow (see Section 4.3) and the attribute is only kept for backward compatibility. **UID** is short for "User ID". The range of the unique numeric value is between 0 and 65535. On Debian, the user root has a UID of 0, services range from 1 to 999, and regular users start at 1000. The image below shows the info for a root user and a regular user.

The **GID** attribute refers to the Group ID for the user's primary group. **GECOS** is short for General Comprehensive Operating System and contains the user's full name and sometimes a comma-separated list of user data like room and telephone number. **Home** is the user's home directory and **shell** is the default shell for the user. To be precise, it is the program that is executed as soon as the user logs in.

/etc/shadow

This file contains the encrypted passwords and expiration data for users. The format is similar to /etc/passwd which we discussed above. Each line consists of eight columns, and the columns are separated by a colon (:). The attributes are the username, the password, the date of the last change, the minimum usage value, the maximum usage value, the warning time, the inactivity period, and the expiration date.

The first attribute **username** again refers to the UNIX username, but in this instance the **password** field does contain the user's encrypted password. **lastchange** indicates the days since 1/1/1970 that the password was last changed. The next two attributes **minimum** and **maximum** show the minimum number of days before the user can change their password, and the maximum number of days the password is still valid. **Warn** shows the number of days prior to the password expiring, that the user will be warned to change the password. The **inactive** attribute is the number of days after expiration until the user is disabled, and the **expiration date** is the number of days after 1/1/1970 since the account has been disabled.

The image below shows the attributes for a regular user. The password is stored as a salted hash value in the second column.

In order to show the account details, invoke the *chage* command followed by the option *-l* (short for --list) along with the username. The image below lists the details for the user named "user".

```
user@debian95: ~
File  Edit  View  Search  Terminal  Help
root@debian95:/home/user# chage -l user
Last password change                                    : Aug 20, 2018
Password expires                                        : never
Password inactive                                       : never
Account expires                                         : never
Minimum number of days between password change          : 0
Maximum number of days between password change          : 99999
Number of days of warning before password expires       : 7
root@debian95:/home/user#
```

As you can see from the above image, the account does not have an expiration date. In order to set this value to 31 December 2019, invoke the *usermod* command with the option *-e* (short for --expiredate) along with the username.

```
# usermod -e 2019-12-31 user
```

To lock and unlock the user account the *usermod* command has two options *-L* (short for --lock) and *-U* (short for --unlock). The next example locks the account for the user named "user". The user can still work and finish his session but is not able to log into the system anymore.

```
# usermod -L user
```

/etc/group

This file contains the user group attributes. Each line consists of four columns, and the columns are separated once again by a colon (:). The attributes are the group name, the password, the group ID and the list of its members. The **groupname** attribute is similar to the username attribute and refers to the UNIX group name, which must be a unique name on the system. The **password** field contains an x because the value has been moved to the file /etc/gshadow, and the field is kept only for backward compatibility.

The **members** attribute provides a comma-separated list of users with access to the group. **GID** is the unique Group ID. The numeric range is between 0 and 65535, with a similar allocation as we have with the UID. The user root has a GID of 0, services range from 1 to 999, and regular users start at 1000. The following code snippet shows this for the root and a regular user.

```
$ grep root /etc/group
root:x:0:
$ egrep "^user" /etc/group
user:x:1000:
$
```

The image below shows the name of the groups which "user" is part of.

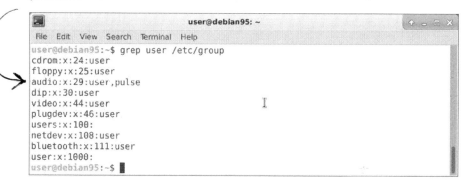

/etc/gshadow

This file contains the encrypted passwords and user data for groups. The format is similar to /etc/shadow. Each line consists of four columns separated by a colon (:). The attributes are the group name, the password, the administrators, and the list of members.

The **groupname** attribute is again the UNIX group name, with the **password** being the encrypted password.

33

Administrators are group members who can add or remove other members using the *gpasswd* command, and **members** are non-administrative members of the group.

4.1 User and Group Commands

There are a number of commands available to manage users and groups in a Linux system. We will look at commands needed to view and change user information, change passwords, create and delete user accounts, as well as look into group commands. Unless stated otherwise, these commands can be run as a regular user.

whoami

This command returns your current user ID as follows:

```
$ whoami
user
$
```

users, who and w

The *users*, *who* and the *w* commands show the users that are currently logged into your Linux system. *w* extends the output of *who* by the uptime information and another column that contains the last command that was executed. In contrast, *users* simply outputs the name of the users as a space-separated list in a single line (see image below).

The single columns for *who* start with the login name of the user. The output is followed by the name of the terminal, where "console" represents a login terminal, and "pts/1" abbreviates the first pseudo terminal session. The last two columns contain the login time and the host the user comes from, in brackets (see image below).

```
user@debian95:~$ who
user     console    2018-08-20 09:36 (:0)
user     pts/2      2018-08-20 09:47 (:0)
user     pts/3      2018-08-20 09:47 (:0)
user@debian95:~$
```

The single columns for *w* contain the login name of the user (titled LOGIN), the name of the terminal (titled TTY), the name of the host the user comes from (titled FROM), the login time (titled LOGIN@), the activity (idle time and CPU usage titled IDLE, JCPU, and PCPU) as well as the last command the user executed (titled WHAT) (see image below).

```
user@debian95:~$ w
 09:49:23 up 9 min,  3 users,  load average: 0.15, 0.03, 0.01
USER     TTY      FROM       LOGIN@   IDLE   JCPU   PCPU WHAT
user     console  :0         09:36    13:14  0.00s  0.04s -:0
user     pts/2    :0         09:47    2:03   0.02s  0.02s xterm
user     pts/3    :0         09:47    2:03   0.01s  0.01s bash
user@debian95:~$
```

id and groups

The *id* command outputs the user and group information of the current user (see image below). From left to right the columns show the user ID (uid=1000(user)), the group id (gid=1000(group)) and the name of the groups the user is a member of.

```
user@debian95:~$ id
uid=1000(user) gid=1000(user) groups=1000(user),24(cdrom),25(floppy),29(audio),3
0(dip),44(video),46(plugdev),108(netdev),111(bluetooth)
user@debian95:~$
```

In order to list the names of all the groups the user belongs to, you can also invoke the *groups* command (see image below). The output is a space-separated list of the group names.

passwd

As described in Chapter 4, the Linux system has at least two users: an administrative root user and a regular user that we simply called "user". Every account is also secured with a password.

In order to change your password, use the *passwd* command from the Debian "passwd" package. As shown below, type in the current password first, press Enter, type in the new password, press Enter to confirm, retype the new password and press Enter to confirm, again.

As a regular user, you are allowed to change your own password only. The administrative root user is able to set a new password for itself and other users as well. In such a scenario, we call *passwd* as follows:

| # passwd felix |
| Changing password for felix. |
| (current) UNIX password: |
| Enter new UNIX password: |

```
Retype new UNIX password:
passwd: password updated successfully
#
```

The password is stored as a hashed value in the configuration file /etc/shadow. The content of this file is only visible to the administrative user. The example below shows how to extract the information for the user "user" with the help of the *grep* command.

chfn

This command is also from the Debian "passwd" package and changes the user information that is stored on your system in the file /etc/passwd. During the installation of your Debian system the basic setup was already done. In order to modify this information you can run *chfn* without further parameters in interactive mode, or with one or more of the following options to adapt only a specific value:

- -f or --full-name: change the full name of the user
- -h or --home-phone: change the home phone of the user
- -r or --room: change the room number of the user
- -w or --work-phone: change the work phone of the user

The following example changes the entry for the home phone number to 135:

```
$ chfn -h 135
Password:
$
```

chsh

This command (also from the Debian "passwd" package) changes the entry for the shell that you use to log into your Linux system. Again, this information is stored in the file /etc/passwd. Which shells are allowed to be used are limited by the entries in the configuration file /etc/shells.

chsh works similar to the *chfn* command. Invoked without further options an interactive method is used (see image below).

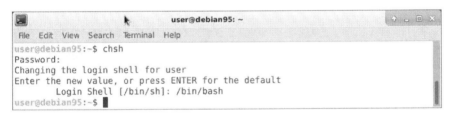

chsh accepts the option *-s* (short for --shell) in order to set the shell in non-interactive mode. The following example shows the command line call:

```
$ chsh -s /bin/bash
$
```

In order to modify the shell for a different user other than yourself, invoke the *chsh* command with the user name as a parameter. Note that only the administrative user can do this for a different user. The next example shows how to do that for the user "felix".

```
# chsh felix
Changing the login shell for felix
Enter the new value, or press ENTER for the new value
    Login shell [/bin/bash]:
#
```

su and sudo

In order to change your role from one user to another, you utilize the *su* command. *su* abbreviates "switch user". Invoked without further options you change to the root user as follows:

```
$ su
Password:
#
```

Working as the administrative root user comes with great responsibility and presumes that you know exactly what you are doing. To work as a different user than root, invoke the *su* command with the desired user name as follows:

```
$ su felix
Password:
$
```

The *su* command changes the current role permanently. In order to run only a single command as an administrative user, use the *sudo* command. This requires the Debian "sudo" package to be installed and the additional user to be added to the configuration file /etc/sudoers using the *visudo* command.

adduser

The command *adduser* creates new user accounts. The image below shows the information that is required. This includes a new entry in the file /etc/passwd as well as the creation of a new group, plus home directory. Furthermore, prepared data from the directory /etc/skel is copied into the previously created home directory. Afterward, the account information is modified using the *chsh* command.

```
root@debian95:~# adduser caro
Adding user `caro' ...
Adding new group `caro' (1002) ...
Adding new user `caro' (1002) with group `caro' ...
Creating home directory `/home/caro' ...
Copying files from `/etc/skel' ...
Enter new UNIX password:
Retype new UNIX password:
passwd: password updated successfully
Changing the user information for caro
Enter the new value, or press ENTER for the default
	Full Name []: Caro
	Room Number []:
	Work Phone []:
	Home Phone []:
	Other []:
Is the information correct? [Y/n] y
root@debian95:~#
```

Having set up the new user, the entry in the file /etc/passwd looks as follows:

```
root@debian95:~# grep caro /etc/passwd
caro:x:1002:1002:Caro,,,:/home/caro:/bin/bash
root@debian95:~#
```

deluser

Deleting user accounts is done with the help of the *deluser* command, while deleting a group can be done via *delgroup*. To delete a user without deleting any of the user's files, use the following command as root user:

```
# deluser felix
```

The *deluser* command has the following options available to fine-tune its execution:

- --group: delete a group, same as *delgroup*

- --system: delete a user only if it is a system user

- --backup: backup the user's files contained in the home directory to a file named /$user.tar.gz or /$user.tar.bz2

- --backup-to: backup the user's files contained in the home directory to a specified file

- --remove-all-files: remove all files from the system that are owned by the user. If a backup is specified, the files will be deleted after performing the backup

    | # deluser --remove-all-files felix |

Free updates on Kindle

I would love your feedback on the content and format of this guide. I use your input to add more value to revisions of this guide, which you will get for free through Kindle updates (remember to claim your free Kindle version of this book if you bought this paperback on Amazon). So let me know what you liked, and what you didn't like so far, through a short review on Amazon. My wife and I read each and every one of them.

5. Filesystems

A filesystem is a way of controlling how data is stored on a drive. If data was not structured, there would be no way of knowing where a particular entry ends and the next one begins. Filesystems separate the data into pieces and each piece has a unique name. This way, information is easily isolated and identified. Each group of data on a filesystem is called an entry. Entries in a filesystem can be files, directories (also named folders), references (also named links), sockets and fifos (also known as named pipes).

Each entry in the filesystem contains the following data:

name
> The name of the entry

permissions
> Which user is the owner of the entry and is allowed to read, write and execute the entry

creation time, last modified time, last access time
> The time the entry was created, modified or accessed last

file size, number of blocks, IO blocks
> How much disk space does the entry need in the filesystem

inode number
> Short for index node and refers to the block number where the data entry starts

number of symlinks
> number of references or symbolic links that point to that entry

You can retrieve the above information by using the *stat* command. *stat* is part of the Debian package "coreutils" and only requires the name of an entry to be examined. The image below displays the information for the file "documentation.pdf".

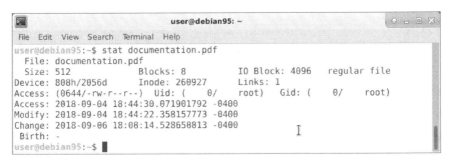

Midnight Commander (mc) also displays this information in a slightly more refined way:

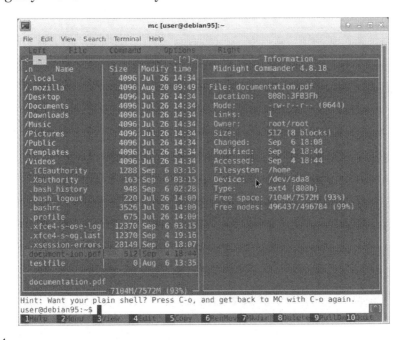

Furthermore, a right click on a file icon that resides on the XFCE desktop opens a properties window in order to show most of the information needed for everyday use:

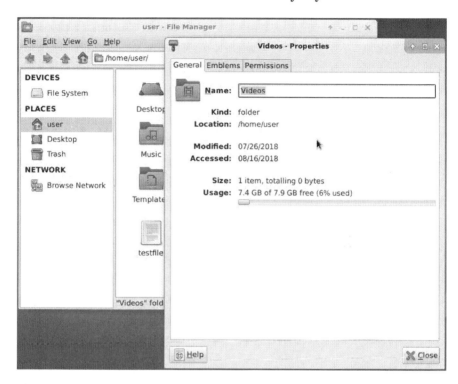

5.1 Types of Commonly Used Filesystems

A number of filesystems are quite popular and widely in use. This includes FAT, ext2, ext3, ext4, JFS, XFS, ZFS, ReiserFS and SWAP. Let's look at them in more detail below.

File Allocation Table (FAT)

FAT was introduced in 1977 for floppy disks and then used for hard disks through the DOS and Microsoft Windows 9X era. It is supported by nearly all operating systems up to the present and useful as a data transfer medium between different systems. It is commonly used on external media such as USB sticks. The original FAT system was only an 8-bit system with a maximum file size of 8MB, supporting 6:3 filenames and no subdirectories. There are 3 main variants of FAT:

- FAT12 - 12 bit File Allocation Table. Supports maximum volume sizes of 16MB with 4KB clusters or 32MB with 8KB clusters.

- FAT16 - 16 bit File Allocation Table. Supports maximum volume sizes of 2GB with 32KB clusters or 4GB with 64KB clusters. Filenames must be in the 8:3 format with OEM characters or 256 UCS characters.

- FAT32 - Supports a maximum file size of 2TB with 512B sectors, 8TB with 2KB sectors and 32K clusters or 16TB with 4KB sectors and 64K clusters. Filenames must be in the 8:3 format with OEM characters or 256 UCS characters.

Second Extended File System (ext2)

This was the first consumer-grade filesystem for Linux and was the default filesystem for Linux distributions such as RedHat and Debian until ext3 became mainstream in 2001. Today, it is still in use on storage devices like digital memory cards, where the journaling functionality of ext3 or ext4 is not needed. This increases performance and minimizes the number of writes.

Third Extended File System (ext3)

Ext3 is a journaled version of ext2 and can be upgraded directly from ext2 without the need for backup and restore operations. Ext3 is not as fast as ext4, JFS, XFS or ReiserFS but it uses less CPU power than ReiserFS or XFS. Ext3 supports files up to 16GB and filesystems up to 32TiB in size.

Fourth Extended File System (ext4)

Ext4 is an extension of ext3 with extra features such as large filesystem support. It supports files up to 16TiB and filesystems up to 1EiB in size. Furthermore, it features extents. An extent is a contiguous range of blocks which makes handling very large files more efficient.

Journaled File System (JFS)

JFS was originally developed for IBM's AIX Unix operating system and later ported to OS/2. JFS is a fully 64bit filesystem which uses extents, supports unlimited small files, and large files up to 4 PB and is ideal for extremely large filesystems.

XFS

XFS is another journaling filesystem developed by Silicon Graphics (SGI) in 1993 for the IRIX operating system. It subdivides physical volumes into allocations allowing more efficient parallel I/O and filesystem bandwidth, and supports large files up to 8EiB.

ZFS

The Zettabyte File System (ZFS) combines a filesystem and a logical volume manager (LVM). Released by SUN Microsystems in 2005, it is scalable and includes extensive protection against data corruption, support for high storage capacities, efficient data compression, integration of filesystem and volume management, snapshots and copy-on-write clones, continuous integrity checking and automatic repair, RAID-Z, and native Access Control Lists (ACLs) for the Network File System (NFS) version 4. The two projects "OpenZFS" and "ZFS on Linux" continue the development of this filesystem.

ReiserFS

ReiserFS is a general-purpose journaled filesystem which uses the Apple Partition Map based on B+Trees for managing directory contents. ReiserFS version 3 was the default filesystem used in SUSE, Elive, Xandros, Linspire, and YOPER distributions. Support for ReiserFS version 4 has declined to the point where development has halted, other than being made compatible with newer Linux kernels.

Swap Space

Swap space is used by Linux to swap out pages of memory when they are not in use. Swap space is not accessible to the user and cannot be used for normal file storage. The space used by swap space is as follows:

- Desktop systems - Use 2x the total amount of memory on the system. That way if many large programs are running concurrently, the unused memory can be saved to disk and programs run more efficiently.

- Server systems - Use 0.5x the total amount of memory. Servers should not be doing a lot of swapping, so half the total memory is enough.

- Old systems with memory less than 1GB - Use as much swap space as possible, as the system will need to do a lot of swapping to run efficiently.

Instead of a separate swap partition, it is also possible to use a swap file. This is created using *dd* to create a fixed size file on an existing partition. This has the advantages of not requiring a fixed swap partition and it can be resized later for efficiency.

5.2 Filesystem Commands

The following commands are used to manage filesystems:

fdisk and cfdisk
> show, create and delete partitions with filesystems on a drive. The image below shows a screen of *cfdisk*.

mkfs
> abbreviation for "make file system" and creates a filesystem.

mkswap
> abbreviation for "make swap" and creates a swap filesystem.

badblocks
> shows bad blocks on a filesystem.

fsck
> abbreviation for "file system check" and examines and repairs a Linux filesystem.

dumpe2fs
> shows information about a filesystem.

link and unlink
> create and delete links to a file.

ln
> abbreviation for "link" and creates hard links and soft links.

ls
> displays information about an entry (file, directory, link, socket or fifo).

lsof
> shows the list of opened files.

stat
   shows all the information that is kept for an entry.

sync
   syncing the drive cache with the disk.

mount and umount
   enabling or disabling a device with a file system.

tune2fs
   adjusts file system parameters on ext2, ext3, and ext4 file systems.

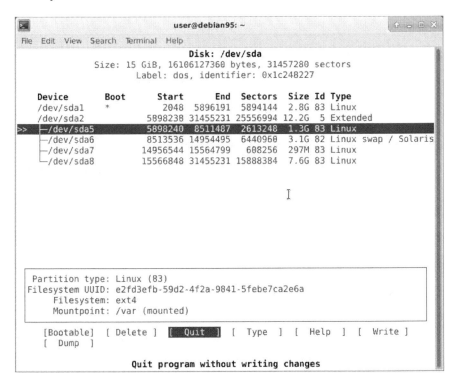

5.3 Practical Example

In the following example, we will look at how to use the commands we mentioned above.

We will emulate a memory disk, create a proper filesystem on it, mount it and store data on it. To start, we will create a file with a size of 10M using *dd* as follows:

```
$ dd if=/dev/zero of=memory.image bs=512b count=40
```

The file consists of zeroes only, as the data is read from a device named /dev/zero that returns zeroes only (if=/dev/zero). The output is written to the file "memory.image" (of=memory.image) with a block size of 512 bytes (bs=512b) forty times (count=40). The image below shows the output of *dd* and the size of the output file using *ls*.

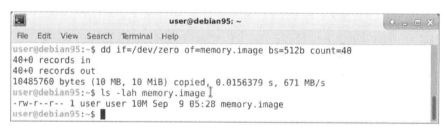

For the next step we create an ext4 filesystem on the file using the command *mkfs.ext4*. The image on the following page shows the outcome.

```
$ /sbin/mkfs.ext4 memory.image 10M
```

This results in a filesystem with 10240 blocks of 1K with space for 2560 entries. Next, we create a mount point using the *mkdir* command:

```
$ mkdir /tmp/image
```

The mount command helps to integrate the image as follows:

```
$ su
Password:
# mount memory.image /tmp/image
#
```

Now we are able to store data on the mounted device. Here, the command *cp* comes into play. In the image below we use *cp -v* to produce additional output.

```
user@debian95: ~
File  Edit  View  Search  Terminal  Help
user@debian95:~$ su
Password:
root@debian95:/home/user# cp -v documentation.pdf /tmp/image/.
'documentation.pdf' -> '/tmp/image/./documentation.pdf'
root@debian95:/home/user# ls /tmp/image/
documentation.pdf  lost+found
root@debian95:/home/user# sync
root@debian95:/home/user# umount /tmp/image
root@debian95:/home/user#
```

Before unmounting the device, issue *sync* to clear the cache and write the data to disk. Finally, we can unmount the filesystem as follows:

```
# umount /tmp/image
# exit
$
```

6. Disk Storage Management

In this chapter we will look at how to deal with storage devices and filesystems, this includes naming the devices, partition types and schemes, as well as mounting and unmounting partitions.

6.1 Naming the Devices

Everything in Linux is a file, a directory is a file and a device is a file too. Every drive on the system is represented as a block device inside the /dev folder. When the system starts up, the "udev" service is run, which detects all devices in /dev and then mounts them accordingly.

Inside /dev, IDE drives have the names "hda", "hdb" all the way up to "hdp". Other device types such as SCSI, USB, SATA, and PATA are represented as "sda", "sdb" up to "sdp". Drives such as CD or DVD drives receive labels like "cdrom" or "dvd" whereas it is common that SD cards are labeled with "mmcblk".

Each drive must have at least one partition if it is to run on the system. A drive can have up to 16 partitions, each with its own filesystem. Within each device, partitions are then labeled "sda1", "sda2" up to "sda16" for the device /dev/sda. Linux has a limit of sixteen drives with sixteen partitions each.

6.2 Primary, Extended, and Logical Partitions

Each drive can have up to four primary partitions, or three primary partitions and one extended partition. Furthermore, an extended partition can contain up to sixteen logical partitions. If a system contains only four primary partitions, they are numbered sda1 through sda4 as follows:

/dev/sda1
/dev/sda2
/dev/sda3
/dev/sda4

If a system contains three primary partitions and one extended partition, which contains logical partitions, primary partition sda4 falls away and is replaced with logical partitions sda5, sda6, sda7 etc:

/dev/sda1
/dev/sda2
/dev/sda3
/dev/sda5
/dev/sda6
/dev/sda7

The first logical partition is always numbered as sda5. So even if there are less than three primary partitions, they are numbered as follows:

/dev/sda1
/dev/sda5
/dev/sda6

In order to see the partition structure, the command *lsblk* from the "util-linux" package is quite helpful. *lsblk* abbreviates "list block devices".

lsblk can output all the block devices that are in use (see first image below) as well as all the unused devices (see second image below).

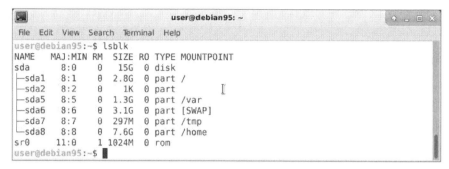

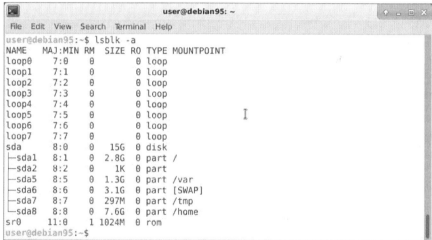

The six columns represent the following information:

NAME

The name of the device.

MAJ:MIN

The major and the minor number of the device.

RM

0 if the device is fixed, and 1 if the device can be removed.

SIZE

The size of the device in a human-readable format.

TYPE

The type of device. "Loop" represents a loop device, "disk" a hard disk, "part" refers to a partition of a disk, "lvm" is a partition run by a Logical Volume Manager (LVM), and "rom" refers to a CD/DVD rom.

MOUNTPOINT

Lists the directory the device is mounted on

To list the mounted filesystems, use either the *mount* command or the *findmnt* command. Both commands are part of the "mount" package. Invoked without further options, *findmnt* prints all the mounted filesystems. This list can be quite long. In order to only select the ext4 filesystems the option *-t ext4* (short for --type ext4) is can be used.

The four output columns contain the following information:

TARGET

The mount point, which is the directory the device is mounted on in the system.

SOURCE

The device name.

FSTYPE

The filesystem type.

OPTIONS

The options which were used to mount the device.

6.3 udev and df

"udev" is the abbreviation for "userspace /dev" and is a device manager for the Linux kernel. Once "udev" runs, the drives it found are shown in the directory /dev/disk. This contains a number of subdirectories with symbolic links as listed below. Note that the number of subdirectories is specific to the Linux release and depends on the version of the Linux kernel. Whenever a disk is recognized by the Linux system, the information is shown here. We can use this information to find which mount points are in use.

/dev/disk/by-id

This shows the partition names that Linux sees and which mount points point to them.

```
# ls -al /dev/disk/by-id
```

```
root@vipserver:~# ls -al /dev/disk/by-id
total 0
drwxr-xr-x 2 root root 220 Sep 5 07:14 .
drwxr-xr-x 7 root root 140 Sep 5 07:14 ..
lrwxrwxrwx 1 root root  9 Sep 5 07:14 ata-VBOX_CD-ROM_VBO-01f00.../sr0
lrwxrwxrwx 1 root root  9 Sep 5 07:14 ata-VBOX_HARDDISK_VBb9372.../sda
lrwxrwxrwx 1 root root 10 Sep 5 07:14 ata-VBOX_HARDDISK...part1.../sda1
lrwxrwxrwx 1 root root 10 Sep 5 07:14 ata-VBOX_HARDDISK...part2.../sda2
lrwxrwxrwx 1 root root 10 Sep 5 07:14 ata-VBOX_HARDDISK...part3.../sda3
lrwxrwxrwx 1 root root 10 Sep 5 07:14 ata-VBOX_HARDDISK...part5.../sda5
lrwxrwxrwx 1 root root 10 Sep 5 07:14 ata-VBOX_HARDDISK...part6.../sda6
lrwxrwxrwx 1 root root 10 Sep 5 07:14 ata-VBOX_HARDDISK...part7.../sda7
lrwxrwxrwx 1 root root  9 Sep 5 07:29 ata-VBOX_HARDDISK_VBc544.../sdb
```

/dev/disk/by-path

This shows lower-level hardware definitions and which mount points mount to them.

```
# ls -al /dev/disk/by-path
```

```
root@vipserver:~# ls -al /dev/disk/by-path
total 0
drwxr-xr-x 2 root root 220 Sep 5 07:14 .
drwxr-xr-x 7 root root 140 Sep 5 07:14 ..
lrwxrwxrwx 1 root root 9 Sep 5 07:14 pci-0000:00:01.1-ata-1.../sr0
lrwxrwxrwx 1 root root 9 Sep 5 07:14 pci-0000:00:0d.0-ata-1.../sda
lrwxrwxrwx 1 root root 10 Sep 5 07:14 pci-0000:00:0d.0...part1.../sda1
lrwxrwxrwx 1 root root 10 Sep 5 07:14 pci-0000:00:0d.0...part2.../sda2
lrwxrwxrwx 1 root root 10 Sep 5 07:14 pci-0000:00:0d.0...part3.../sda3
lrwxrwxrwx 1 root root 10 Sep 5 07:14 pci-0000:00:0d.0...part5.../sda5
lrwxrwxrwx 1 root root 10 Sep 5 07:14 pci-0000:00:0d.0...part6.../sda6
lrwxrwxrwx 1 root root 10 Sep 5 07:14 pci-0000:00:0d.0...part7.../sda7
lrwxrwxrwx 1 root root 9 Sep 5 07:29 pci-0000:00:0d.0-ata-2.../sdb
```

/dev/disk/by-label

This shows which labels are applied to which mount points.

```
# ls -al /dev/disk/by-label
```

```
root@vipserver:~# ls -al /dev/disk/by-label
total 0
drwxr-xr-x 2 root root 220 Sep 5 07:14 .
drwxr-xr-x 7 root root 140 Sep 5 07:14 ..
lrwxrwxrwx 1 root root 10 Sep 5 07:14 home -> ../../sda7
lrwxrwxrwx 1 root root 10 Sep 5 07:14 root -> ../../sda1
lrwxrwxrwx 1 root root 10 Sep 5 07:14 tmp -> ../../sda5
lrwxrwxrwx 1 root root 10 Sep 5 07:14 var -> ../../sda6
```

/dev/disk/by-uuid

This shows the UUID labels for each mount point.

```
# ls -al /dev/disk/by-uuid
```

```
root@vipserver:~# ls -al /dev/disk/by-uuid
total 0
drwxr-xr-x 2 root root 140 Sep  5 07:14 .
drwxr-xr-x 7 root root 140 Sep  5 07:14 ..
lrwxrwxrwx 1 root root  10 Sep  5 07:14 9ef7106a-c885-4cbe-aaa1.../sda2
lrwxrwxrwx 1 root root  10 Sep  5 07:14 ac2823cc-a7b4-4bf3-808e.../sda7
lrwxrwxrwx 1 root root  10 Sep  5 07:14 d2f4fd43-4f76-414c-9afa.../sda6
lrwxrwxrwx 1 root root  10 Sep  5 07:14 dc78e6f6-8a4f-4be0-9192.../sda1
lrwxrwxrwx 1 root root  10 Sep  5 07:14 faef6770-b865-43d2-b1f6.../sda5
```

/dev/disk/by-partuuid is a component of GUID Partition Tables (GPT) which is a replacement for Master Boot Record (MBR) related disk partitioning.

df

To see which filesystems are mounted, and how many blocks are used and available, invoke the *df* command. *df* is an abbreviation for "disk free". The command offers various options:

- df -h: List in a human-readable format.
- df -k: List in kilobytes.
- df -m: List in megabytes.
- df: List in default block size. Sometimes this uses 500KB which can be confusing.

```
root@vipserver:~# df -k
Filesystem     1K-blocks      Used  Available Use% Mounted on
udev             1015136         0    1015136   0% /dev
tmpfs             205256      2984     202272   2% /run
/dev/sda1        3778616   1628296    1938660  46% /
tmpfs            1026268         0    1026268   0% /dev/shm
tmpfs               5120         0       5120   0% /run/lock
tmpfs            1026268         0    1026268   0% /sys/fs/cgroup
/dev/sda5         463826      2316     433043   1% /tmp
/dev/sda7       15035192    327488   13924244   3% /home
/dev/sda6        9545920    461072    8580224   6% /var
tmpfs             205252         0     205252   0% /run/user/1000
```

6.4 Mounting a Filesystem

Before a filesystem can be used, it must be mounted as part of the directory tree. Most of the time, this is done automatically at startup but can also be done manually. We briefly looked at the commands used for manual mounting at the end of the previous chapter, but we will go into more detail on their usage here.

To demonstrate, we will mount the first partition of the second SCSI disk (/deb/sdb1) as /space. Firstly, in order to mount a filesystem you must be in root. Next, if the directory /space does not exist yet, create it using *mkdir* as follows:

```
# mkdir /space
```

Then run the *mount* command to include this directory:

```
# mount /dev/sdb1 /space
```

Most of the time Linux detects the filesystem type automatically. If this is not the case and the type is not detected automatically, use the *-t* parameter (short for --type) followed by the name of the filesystem type to force it. This step assumes that the relevant filesystem type is installed and recognized by the Linux kernel. To list all the filesystems supported by the Linux kernel, the combination of the commands *cat, awk, sed, ls* and *sort* can be used as follows:

```
$ (cat /proc/filesystems | awk '{print $NF}' | sed '/^$/d'; ls -1 /lib/modules/$(uname -r)/ -
kernel/fs) | sort -u
9p
adfs
affs
afs
aufs
```

```
autofs
autofs4
bdev
befs
bfs
binfmt_misc
binfmt_misc.ko
btrfs
cachefiles
ceph...
$
```

The following command extends the commands from above in order to mount the first partition of the second SCSI disk (/deb/ sdb1) as /space using an ext3 filesystem [ext3]:

```
# mount -t ext3 /dev/sdb1 /space
```

6.5 Unmounting a Filesystem

If the filesystem is busy or in use, it cannot be unmounted. To find out which programs are using the filesystem the *lsof* command from the "lsof" package comes into play. *lsof* abbreviates "list of open files". The image below demonstrates how to use the command, and shows this for the directory /home/user/Music.

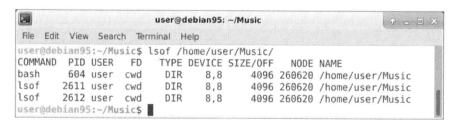

This gives a list of programs using the directory. Also if a user is working in that directory, that counts as well, and you will have to change directory with the *cd* command.

To unmount the directory /space which we mounted in the previous section, you must again be in root. Next, test if any other programs are using /space by invoking the command *lsof /space*. If any programs are running, stop them and try again. Also, make sure that no terminals are cd'd into /space.

```
$ su
Password:
# lsof /space
...
```

Then type *umount /space*. If you do not get an error message, then /space was successfully unmounted. Alternatively, run the *umount* command with the option *-v* (short for --verbose) in order to see the transaction message. Finally, type *df - k* to see the new partition state.

```
...
# umount /space
# exit
$
```

6.6 Automating Mount Points

To automatically mount a mount point during startup of your Linux system, add an entry in the configuration file /etc/fstab. *fstab* abbreviates "file system table". The image below displays the content of the configuration file.

```
root@vipserver:~# cat /etc/fstab
# /etc/fstab: static file system information.
#
# Use 'blkid' to print the universally unique identifier for a
# device; this may be used with UUID= as a more robust way to name
# devices that works even if disks are added and removed. See
# fstab(5).
#
```

```
# <file system>           <mount point><type><options><dump><pass>
# / was on /dev/sda1 during installation
UUID=dc78e6f6-8a4f-4be0-9192-e4ca37838765   /       ext4   errors=   0 1
# /home was on /dev/sda7 during installation
UUID=ac2823cc-a7b4-4bf3-808e-e13401e11eaf   /home ext4   defaults  0 2
# /tmp was on /dev/sda5 during installation
UUID=faef6770-b865-43d2-b1f6-56352413d7c4   /tmp    ext4   defaults  0 2
# /var was on /dev/sda6 during installation
UUID=d2f4fd43-4f76-414c-9afa-6a53d4cd1d9c   /var    ext4   defaults  0 2
# swap was on /dev/sda2 during installation
UUID=9ef7106a-c885-4cbe-aaa1-8e2b77ee73cf   none   swap   sw        0 0
/dev/sr0     /media/cdrom0    udf,iso9660 user,noauto   0 0
```

The columns (fields) in the file /etc/fstab are:

filesystem
Specifies the UUID (UUID=xxxxx), name (/dev/sdb1), or the label of the filesystem (LABEL=home).

mount point
Defines the directory where the filesystem will be mounted.

type
A comma-separated list of allowed filesystem types.

options
A comma-separated list of options.

dump
Dump information in file with 0 = off, and 1 = on

pass
The order the filesystem is checked starting with 1. 0 means last

Keep in mind that the single columns are separated by a tabulator, and spaces do not work properly. Tip: to find the UUID for the mount point, look in /dev/disk/by-uuid.

To add a device to mount automatically, extend the file /etc/fstab by simply adding a line. In order to mount the partition /dev/sdb1 as /space with an ext3 filesystem at startup, add this line on older systems:

```
/dev/sdb1 /space ext3 defaults 0 0
```

On contemporary systems that support UUIDs, use the following line. Note to replace the value of "7ca005b2-a7ff-4757-bfdf-81004d4 072ef" by the real UUID of the partition:

```
UUID=7ca005b2-a7ff-4757-bfdf-81004d4072ef /space ext3 defaults 0 0
```

Now /dev/sdb1 will always be mounted as /space at startup. You may wonder what the advantage is of using a UUID.

By using a UUID the partition is clearly identified, even if the order of the disks changes later on.

In order to generate a UUID (or to regenerate a new one) use the *uuidgen* command line tool. It offers two options. The first is *-r* (short for --random) which generates a random-based UUID. This method creates a UUID consisting mostly of random bits. This is the default value if not explicitly specified.

```
$ uuidgen -r
4d545248-cf36-4d24-91ab-64a9ed276072
$
```

The second option is -t (short for --time) which generates a time-based UUID. This method creates an UUID based on the system clock plus the system's ethernet hardware address, if present.

```
$ uuidgen -t
4afa1166-bcf1-11e8-9a0a-68f728ff3d63
$
```

The *uuidgen* command writes the newly generated UUID to "stdout". You can copy and paste the new UUID directly into /etc/fstab to have a unique identifier for a partition to be referenced.

6.7 Setting up New Partitions

The idea behind *fdisk* and its counterparts, *cfdisk* and *gparted,* is to view the partitions on a disk and to add, remove or edit partitions. In this section we will have a look at *fdisk*, which is a standard package for Debian and is also available on all major Linux distributions. Both *cfdisk* and *gparted* are non-standard packages and may require separate installation.

In order to use *fdisk,* as root user type *fdisk* followed by the name of the drive. The next example shows this for the first SCSI disk named /dev/sda:

```
# fdisk /dev/sda
```

This will open a screen as shown below. At the command line prompt press *p* in order to print the partitions:

```
root@vipserver:~# fdisk /dev/sda

Welcome to fdisk (util-linux 2.29.2).
Changes will remain in memory only, until you decide to write them.
Be careful before using the write command.
```

```
Command (m for help): p
Disk /dev/sda: 30 GiB, 32212254720 bytes, 62914560 sectors
Units: sectors of 1 * 512 = 512 bytes
Sector size (logical/physical): 512 bytes / 512 bytes
I/O size (minimum/optimal): 512 bytes / 512 bytes
Disklabel type: dos
Disk identifier: 0x2e4f25d8

Device     Boot     Start       End   Sectors  Size  Id  Type
/dev/sda1   *        2048   7813119   7811072  3.7G  83  Linux
/dev/sda2         7813120  11718655   3905536  1.9G  82  Linux swap
/dev/sda3        11720702  62912511  51191810 24.4G   5  Extended
/dev/sda5        11720704  12695551    974848  476M  83  Linux
/dev/sda6        12697600  32227327  19529728  9.3G  83  Linux
/dev/sda7        32229376  62912511  30683136 14.6G  83  Linux
```

To get a list of commands available, type *m*, and the following screen (shown on the next page) will appear. Use *q* to quit *fdisk*.

```
Command (m for help): m
Help:

  DOS (MBR)
   a   toggle a bootable flag
   b   edit nested BSD disklabel
   c   toggle the dos compatibility flag
  Generic
   d   delete a partition
   F   list free unpartitioned space
   l   list known partition types
   n   add a new partition
   p   print the partition table
   t   change a partition type
   v   verify the partition table
   i   print information about a partition
  Misc
   m   print this menu
   u   change display/entry units
   x   extra functionality (experts only)
```

```
Script
  I    load disk layout from sfdisk script file
  O    dump disk layout to sfdisk script file
Save & Exit
  w    write table to disk and exit
  q    quit without saving changes
Create a new label
  g    create a new empty GPT partition table
  G    create a new empty SGI (IRIX) partition table
  o    create a new empty DOS partition table
  s    create a new empty Sun partition table
```

Creating New Partitions

For the second SCSI disk, start *fdisk* as follows:

```
# fdisk /dev/sdb
```

To create a new partition type "n", first *fdisk* asks us if we would like to create a primary partition or an extended partition. We select *p* for a primary partition.

Then *fdisk* asks us what partition number we want. We select *1* for the first partition. Next, it asks for the size. By default *fdisk* fills the entire disk and uses the entire space that is available. We select *+4GB* for a 4GB partition. Then we type *p* to print out the result and we can see the partition /dev/sdb1 has been created.

```
Command (m for help): n
Partition type
   p   primary (0 primary, 0 extended, 4 free)
   e   extended (container for logical partitions)
Select (default p): p
Partition number (1-4, default 1): 1
First sector (2048-41943039, default 2048):
Last sector, +sectors or +size{K,M,G,T,P} (2048-41943039, default
      41943039): +4G
Created a new partition 1 of type 'Linux' and of size 4 GiB.
```

```
Command (m for help): p
Disk /dev/sdb: 20 GiB, 21474836480 bytes, 41943040 sectors
Units: sectors of 1 * 512 = 512 bytes
Sector size (logical/physical): 512 bytes / 512 bytes
I/O size (minimum/optimal): 512 bytes / 512 bytes
Disklabel type: dos
Disk identifier: 0x056efeb2

Device     Boot  Start     End  Sectors  Size  Id  Type
/dev/sdb1        2048  8390655  8388608   4G   83  Linux
```

Now let us add an extended partition. Again, type *n* to create a new partition. This time from the menu we select *e* for an extended partition and hit enter for the default settings, partition 2 and fill all the remaining space. Then type *p* to print out the result and we can see the extended partition /dev/sdb2 has been created.

```
Command (m for help): n
Partition type
   p   primary (1 primary, 0 extended, 3 free)
   e   extended (container for logical partitions)
Select (default p): e
Partition number (2-4, default 2):
First sector (8390656-41943039, default 8390656):
Last sector, +sectors or +size{K,M,G,T,P} (8390656-41943039, default
     41943039):
Created a new partition 2 of type 'Extended' and of size 16 GiB.

Command (m for help): p
Disk /dev/sdb: 20 GiB, 21474836480 bytes, 41943040 sectors
Units: sectors of 1 * 512 = 512 bytes
Sector size (logical/physical): 512 bytes / 512 bytes
I/O size (minimum/optimal): 512 bytes / 512 bytes
Disklabel type: dos
Disk identifier: 0x056efeb2

Device     Boot     Start       End   Sectors  Size  Id  Type
/dev/sdb1            2048   8390655   8388608   4G   83  Linux
/dev/sdb2         8390656  41943039  33552384  16G    5  Extended
```

Now let's create a swap space. Again, type *n* to create a new partition. This time there is no more room for a primary partition, so we can only create a logical partition. We use the default First Sector and select *+1G* for the Last Sector and hit enter for the defaults. Type *p* to see the result and we can see that logical partition /dev/sdb5 has been created. Type *f* to show how much free space is still available on the drive.

```
Command (m for help): n
All space for primary partitions is in use.
Adding logical partition 5
First sector (8392704-41943039, default 8392704):
Last sector, +sectors or +size{K,M,G,T,P} (8392704-41943039, default
    41943039): +1G
Created a new partition 5 of type 'Linux' and of size 1 GiB.

Command (m for help): p
Disk /dev/sdb: 20 GiB, 21474836480 bytes, 41943040 sectors
Units: sectors of 1 * 512 = 512 bytes
Sector size (logical/physical): 512 bytes / 512 bytes
I/O size (minimum/optimal): 512 bytes / 512 bytes
Disklabel type: dos
Disk identifier: 0x056efeb2

Device     Boot    Start        End    Sectors   Size  Id  Type
/dev/sdb1          2048      8390655   8388608    4G   83  Linux
/dev/sdb2       8390656     41943039  33552384   16G    5  Extended
/dev/sdb5       8392704     10489855   2097152    1G   83  Linux

Command (m for help): F
Unpartitioned space /dev/sdb:
    15 GiB, 16102981632 bytes, 31451136 sectors
Units: sectors of 1 * 512 = 512 bytes
Sector size (logical/physical): 512 bytes / 512 bytes

   Start         End    Sectors   Size
10491904    41943039   31451136    15G
```

Finally, let's create one partition using all the free space. We do the same as with the last partition, except this time we select all the default options. Typing *p* afterward shows us partition /dev/sdb6 has been created.

```
Command (m for help): n
All space for primary partitions is in use.
Adding logical partition 6
First sector (10491904-41943039, default 10491904):
Last sector, +sectors or +size{K,M,G,T,P} (10491904-41943039,
      default 41943039):

Created a new partition 6 of type 'Linux' and of size 15 GiB.

Command (m for help): p
Disk /dev/sdb: 20 GiB, 21474836480 bytes, 41943040 sectors
Units: sectors of 1 * 512 = 512 bytes
Sector size (logical/physical): 512 bytes / 512 bytes
I/O size (minimum/optimal): 512 bytes / 512 bytes
Disklabel type: dos
Disk identifier: 0x056efeb2

Device      Boot    Start       End   Sectors  Size Id Type
/dev/sdb1           2048    8390655   8388608   4G  83 Linux
/dev/sdb2        8390656   41943039  33552384  16G   5 Extended
/dev/sdb5        8392704   10489855   2097152   1G  83 Linux
/dev/sdb6       10491904   41943039  31451136  15G  83 Linux
```

Now let's change the partition /dev/sdb5 to a swap space. To do this, in *fdisk* type *t* to change the partition type. For partition number we select *5*, and then type *l* to list the available types. The type we want is Linux swap / Solaris. Type *p* to show that the partition's type has changed.

```
Command (m for help): t
Partition number (1,2,5,6,default 6): 5
Partition type (type L to list all types): L
```

```
 0 Empty                24 NEC DOS              81 Minix / old Lin
 1 FAT12                27 Hidden NTFS Win      82 Linux swap / So
 2 XENIX root           39 Plan 9               83 Linux
 3 XENIX usr            3c PartitionMagic       84 OS/2 hidden or
 4 FAT16 <32M           40 Venix 80286          85 Linux extended
 5 Extended             41 PPC PReP Boot        86 NTFS volume set
 6 FAT16                42 SFS                  87 NTFS volume set
 7 HPFS/NTFS/exFAT      4d QNX4.x               88 Linux plaintext
 8 AIX                  4e QNX4.x 2nd part      8e Linux LVM
 9 AIX bootable         4f QNX4.x 3rd part      93 Amoeba
 a OS/2 Boot Manag      50 OnTrack DM           94 Amoeba BBT
 b W95 FAT32            51 OnTrack DM6 Aux      9f BSD/OS
 c W95 FAT32 (LBA)      52 CP/M                 a0 IBM Thinkpad hi
 e W95 FAT16 (LBA)      53 OnTrack DM6 Aux      a5 FreeBSD
 f W95 Ext'd (LBA)      54 OnTrackDM6           a6 OpenBSD
10 OPUS                 55 EZ-Drive             a7 NeXTSTEP
11 Hidden FAT12         56 Golden Bow           a8 Darwin UFS
12 Compaq diagnost      5c Priam Edisk          a9 NetBSD
Partition type (type L to list all types): 82

Changed type of partition 'Linux' to 'Linux swap / Solaris'.

Command (m for help): p
Disk /dev/sdb: 20 GiB, 21474836480 bytes, 41943040 sectors
Units: sectors of 1 * 512 = 512 bytes
Sector size (logical/physical): 512 bytes / 512 bytes
I/O size (minimum/optimal): 512 bytes / 512 bytes
Disklabel type: dos
Disk identifier: 0x056efeb2

Device     Boot    Start       End   Sectors  Size  Id  Type
/dev/sdb1           2048   8390655   8388608    4G  83  Linux
/dev/sdb2        8390656  41943039  33552384   16G   5  Extended
/dev/sdb5        8392704  10489855   2097152    1G  82  Linux swap
/dev/sdb6       10491904  41943039  31451136   15G  83  Linux
```

Up to now, nothing has been written to disk. To do this, we need to save and sync disks by typing *w* to write to disk.

Now we exit *fdisk* by typing *q* to quit. Type *ls -al /dev/disk/by-id* to see the newly created partitions. As the next step, we will use the newly created partitions to mount filesystems.

```
root@vipserver:~# ls -al /dev/disk/by-id
total 0
drwxr-xr-x 2 root root 300 Sep  5 12:54 .
drwxr-xr-x 7 root root 140 Sep  5 07:14 ..
lrwxrwxrwx 1 root root  9 Sep  5 07:14 ata-VBOX_CD-ROM_VBO-01f00.../sr0
lrwxrwxrwx 1 root root  9 Sep  5 07:14 ata-VBOX_HARDDISK_VBb9372.../sda
lrwxrwxrwx 1 root root 10 Sep  5 07:14 ata-VBOX_HARDDISK...part1.../sda1
lrwxrwxrwx 1 root root 10 Sep  5 07:14 ata-VBOX_HARDDISK...part2.../sda2
lrwxrwxrwx 1 root root 10 Sep  5 07:14 ata-VBOX_HARDDISK...part3.../sda3
lrwxrwxrwx 1 root root 10 Sep  5 07:14 ata-VBOX_HARDDISK...part5.../sda5
lrwxrwxrwx 1 root root 10 Sep  5 07:14 ata-VBOX_HARDDISK...part6.../sda6
lrwxrwxrwx 1 root root 10 Sep  5 07:14 ata-VBOX_HARDDISK...part7.../sda7
lrwxrwxrwx 1 root root  9 Sep  5 12:54 ata-VBOX_HARDDISK_VBc544.../sdb
lrwxrwxrwx 1 root root 10 Sep  5 12:54 ata-VBOX_HARDDISK...part1.../sdb1
lrwxrwxrwx 1 root root 10 Sep  5 12:54 ata-VBOX_HARDDISK...part2.../sdb2
lrwxrwxrwx 1 root root 10 Sep  5 12:54 ata-VBOX_HARDDISK...part5.../sdb5
lrwxrwxrwx 1 root root 10 Sep  5 12:54 ata-VBOX_HARDDISK...part6.../sdb6
```

Creating New Filesystems

So far we have empty partitions only. These partitions need to be filled with the appropriate filesystems. We will mount the new filesystems as follows:

```
/dev/sdb1 /mnt/root ext2
/dev/sdb5 swap
/dev/sdb6 /mnt/home ext4
```

To do this, first we create the mount points that we need:

```
# mkdir /mnt/root
# mkdir /mnt/home
```

Then to add the filesystems, we issue the following commands:

```
# mkfs /dev/sdb1
# mkfs.ext4 /dev/sdb6
```

```
root@vipserver:~# mkfs /dev/sdb1
mke2fs 1.43.4 (31-Jan-2017)
Creating filesystem with 1048576 4k blocks and 262144 inodes
Filesystem UUID: 8e70eeac-83cb-43f1-a402-a10fdecab950
Superblock backups stored on blocks:
    32768,98304,163840,229376,294912,819200,884736

Allocating group tables: done
Writing inode tables: done
Writing superblocks and filesystem accounting information: done

root@vipserver:~# mkfs.ext4 /dev/sdb6
mke2fs 1.43.4 (31-Jan-2017)
Creating filesystem with 3931392 4k blocks and 983040 inodes
Filesystem UUID: e7ab67d6-53a6-4c1a-9ee2-5f36d183bef5
Superblock backups stored on blocks:
    32768,98304,163840,229376,294912,819200,884736,1605632,2654208

Allocating group tables: done
Writing inode tables: done
Creating journal (16384 blocks): done
Writing superblocks and filesystem accounting information: done
```

Next, we have to set up /dev/sdb5 as a swap partition. *mkswap* creates a swap filesystem, and *swapon* activates the partition as swap space.

```
# mkswap /dev/sdb5
# swapon /dev/sdb5
```

```
root@vipserver:~# mkswap /dev/sdb5
Setting up swapspace version 1, size = 1024 MiB (1073737728 bytes)
no label, UUID=a6e9f014-500b-4659-a45f-86d09238d11c
root@vipserver:~# swapon /dev/sdb5
```

It is a good idea to give each partition its own label. To do this we use *tune2fs* in combination with its option -L. The partition /dev/sdb1 is associated with the directory /root, and the partition /dev/sdb6 is associated with the directory /home.

```
# tune2fs -L root /dev/sdb1
# tune2fs -L home /dev/sdb6
```

Now we can mount the new partitions. Type *df* to see the result.

```
root@vipserver:~# mkdir /mnt/root
root@vipserver:~# mkdir /mnt/home
root@vipserver:~# mount /dev/sdb1 /mnt/root
root@vipserver:~# mount /dev/sdb6 /mnt/home
root@vipserver:~#
root@vipserver:~# df
Filesystem     1K-blocks      Used  Available  Use% Mounted on
udev             1015136         0    1015136    0% /dev
tmpfs             205256      3008     202248    2% /run
/dev/sda1        3778616   1628304    1938652   46% /
tmpfs            1026268         0    1026268    0% /dev/shm
tmpfs               5120         0       5120    0% /run/lock
tmpfs            1026268         0    1026268    0% /sys/fs/cgroup
/dev/sda5         463826      2316     433043    1% /tmp
/dev/sda7       15035192    327488   13924244    3% /home
/dev/sda6        9545920    461356    8579940    6% /var
tmpfs             205252         0     205252    0% /run/user/1000
/dev/sdb1        4128448      8184    3910552    1% /mnt/root
/dev/sdb6       15413192     40984   14569548    1% /mnt/home
```

As the final step let us add entries to the configuration file /etc/fstab in order to be able to auto-mount these filesystems at startup. First make a copy of /etc/fstab as /etc/fstab.bak:

```
# cp /etc/fstab /etc/fstab.bak
```

Then in order to get the block IDs of the new partitions, type *lsblk -f*. The option *-f* (short for --fs) extends the output with additional filesystem information.

```
root@vipserver:/etc# lsblk -f
NAME    FSTYPE  LABEL   UUID                                    MOUNTPOINT
sda
-sda1   ext4    root    dc78e6f6-8a4f-4be0-9192-e4ca37838765    /
-sda2   swap            9ef7106a-c885-4cbe-aaa1-8e2b77ee73cf    [SWAP]
-sda3
-sda5   ext4    tmp     faef6770-b865-43d2-b1f6-56352413d7c4    /tmp
-sda6   ext4    var     d2f4fd43-4f76-414c-9afa-6a53d4cd1d9c    /var
-sda7   ext4    home    ac2823cc-a7b4-4bf3-808e-e13401e11eaf    /home
sdb
-sdb1   ext2    root    8e70eeac-83cb-43f1-a402-a10fdecab950    /mnt/root
-sdb2
-sdb5   swap            a6e9f014-500b-4659-a45f-86d09238d11c    [SWAP]
-sdb6   ext4    home    e7ab67d6-53a6-4c1a-9ee2-5f36d183bef5    /mnt/home
```

Now edit the configuration file /etc/fstab and add the last two lines as shown in the image below (/mnt/root & /mnt/home).

```
root@vipserver:/etc# cat fstab
# /etc/fstab: static file system information.
#
# Use 'blkid' to print the universally unique identifier for a
# device; this may be used with UUID= as a more robust way to name
# devices that works even if disks are added and removed. See
# fstab(5).
#
# <file system>              <mount point><type><options><dump><pass>
# / was on /dev/sda1 during installation
UUID=dc78e6f6-8a4f-4be0-9192-e4ca37838765  /       ext4    errors=   0 1
# /home was on /dev/sda7 during installation
UUID=ac2823cc-a7b4-4bf3-808e-e13401e11eaf  /home ext4   defaults   0 2
# /tmp was on /dev/sda5 during installation
UUID=faef6770-b865-43d2-b1f6-56352413d7c4  /tmp    ext4    defaults  0 2
# /var was on /dev/sda6 during installation
UUID=d2f4fd43-4f76-414c-9afa-6a53d4cd1d9c  /var    ext4    defaults  0 2
```

```
# swap was on /dev/sda2 during installation
UUID=9ef7106a-c885-4cbe-aaa1-8e2b77ee73cf  none  swap  sw         0 0
/dev/sr0    /media/cdrom0    udf,iso9660 user,noauto  0 0

UUID=8e70eeac-83cb-43f1-a402-a10fdecab950 /mnt/root ext2 default 0 2
UUID=e7ab67d6-53a6-4c1a-9ee2-5f36d183bef5 /mnt/home ext4 default 0 2
```

Then restart the system with your new partitions using *reboot*, and invoke *df* in order to see the newly created partitions.

```
jk@vipserver:~$ df
Filesystem     1K-blocks       Used  Available  Use% Mounted on
udev             1015136          0    1015136    0% /dev
tmpfs             205256       3000     202256    2% /run
/dev/sda1        3778616    1628304    1938652   46% /
tmpfs            1026268          0    1026268    0% /dev/shm
tmpfs               5120          0       5120    0% /run/lock
tmpfs            1026268          0    1026268    0% /sys/fs/cgroup
/dev/sdb1        4128448       8184    3910552    1% /mnt/root
/dev/sda7       15035192     327488   13924244    3% /home
/dev/sdb6       15413192      40984   14569548    1% /mnt/home
/dev/sda5         463826       2316     433043    1% /tmp
/dev/sda6        9545920     461532    8579764    6% /var
tmpfs             205252          0     205252    0% /run/user/1000
```

> ***Learned something new?***
>
> If you found any part of this guide helpful so far, or learned something new that you can't wait to try out, I would love to hear about it. The main way for me to connect with you, is through a review on Amazon. So head over there and let me know which topics you liked most, or even which ones you didn't like. Are you using this guide in your studies or job? I would love to hear about it as well.
>
>

7. Working with Links

There are two kinds of links in a Linux filesystem: hard links and soft links. We will explain both of them in more detail below.

7.1 Hard Links

A hard link links a filename to the place on the drive where the file is stored (reference to an inode). It is merely an additional name for an existing file. Each file can have more than one hard link, but it must have at least one. If no links to the file exist, the file is deleted and the space on the drive is freed up for other files. However, the data in the file is still there and can be recovered as long as it is not written over.

Every filename on the system is a hard link. Hard links cannot point to directories, soft links, characters or block devices, pipes or sockets. If more than one hard link points to a file, they must be on the same filesystem. To create a link Linux utilizes two commands: *link* and *ln*. The *link* command is used solely for hard links. It calls the "link()" system function and does not perform error checking when attempting to create the link. In contrast, *ln* has error checking and can create both hard and soft links.

The following command creates three hard links named "link1", "link2" and "link3" to the file "test":

```
$ touch test
$ ln test link1
$ ln test link2
$ ln test link3
$
```

The output of *ls -i* shows two columns: the inode number and the filename (*-i* is short for *-inode*). You can see that the inode number is the same for the four files, and link1, link2, link3 and test point to the same inode.

```
$ ls -i test link*
260930 link1
260930 link2
260930 link3
260930 test
$
```

Furthermore, the *stat* command gives more detailed information about the entry.

```
user@debian95:~$ touch test
user@debian95:~$ ln test link1
user@debian95:~$ ln test link2
user@debian95:~$ ln test link3
user@debian95:~$ stat test
  File: test
  Size: 0         Blocks: 0          IO Block: 4096   regular empty file
Device: 808h/2056d    Inode: 260930      Links: 4
Access: (0644/-rw-r--r--)  Uid: ( 1000/    user)   Gid: ( 1000/    user)
Access: 2018-09-19 16:51:10.033912519 +0200
Modify: 2018-09-19 16:51:10.033912519 +0200
Change: 2018-09-19 16:51:19.245900960 +0200
 Birth: -
user@debian95:~$
```

7.2 Soft Links

A soft link, also named a symbolic link, is a link to another filename in the filesystem. It is much like a shortcut.

Unlike a hard link, a symbolic link does not contain the data in the target file, it simply points to another entry somewhere in the filesystem. This difference gives symbolic links certain qualities that hard links do not have, such as the ability to link to directories, characters, block devices, or to files on remote computers networked through NFS.

To create a soft link in Linux, we will use the same *ln* utility but with the *-s* option. *-s* is short for *--symbolic*.

```
$ touch test
$ ln -s test softlink1
$ ln -s test softlink2
$ ln -s test soft link3
$
```

Again, the output of *ls -i* shows two columns: the inode number and the filename. You will see that the inode number is different for the four files, and softlink1, softlink2, softlink3, and test point to different inodes.

```
$ ls -i test softlink*
260931 softlink1
260932 softlink2
260933 softlink3
260930 test
$
```

If you invoke the *ls* command with the option *-l* (for long format) the output is as shown below. The left-most column starts with an "l" for link, and the right-most column shows the name of the file the soft link points to.

79

```
$ ls -l softlink*
lrwxrwxrwx 1 user user 4 Sep 15 14:05 softlink1 -> test
lrwxrwxrwx 1 user user 4 Sep 15 14:05 softlink2 -> test
lrwxrwxrwx 1 user user 4 Sep 15 14:05 softlink3 -> test
$
```

7.3 Practical Example

In this example we will look at how to connect two files using links, and how to unlink them again. First, create a file "file1" using *echo* and redirecting the output.

```
$ echo "This is File One" > file1
$ cat file1
This is File One
$
```

Next, link "file2" to "file1" and output the contents of "file2" to *stdout*.

```
$ link file1 file2
$ cat file2
This is File One
$
```

Now they are both the same file. Let's make a change to "file2" and see what happens.

```
$ echo "This is line Two" >> file2
$ cat file1
This is File One
This is line Two
$
```

As you can see from the image below, "file1" and "file2" are both treated as the same file.

```
jk@vipserver:~/test$ ls -l
total 0
jk@vipserver:~/test$ echo "This is File One" > file1
jk@vipserver:~/test$ cat file1
This is File One
jk@vipserver:~/test$ link file1 file2
jk@vipserver:~/test$ ls
file1 file2
jk@vipserver:~/test$ cat file2
This is File One
jk@vipserver:~/test$ echo "This is line Two" >> file2
jk@vipserver:~/test$ cat file2
This is File One
This is line Two
jk@vipserver:~/test$ cat file1
This is File One
This is line Two
```

Unlinking "file1" deletes the hard link to "file1" but "file2" is still there and the file will not be deleted.

```
$ unlink file1
$ ls
file2
$
```

Unlinking "file2" deletes the hard link to "file2" and also deletes the file. The file no longer exists and the space it took up on the hard drive is marked for overwriting.

```
$ unlink file2
$ ls
$
```

```
jk@vipserver:~/test$ unlink file1
jk@vipserver:~/test$ ls
file2
jk@vipserver:~/test$ cat file2
This is File One
This is line Two
jk@vipserver:~/test$ unlink file2
jk@vipserver:~/test$ ls
jk@vipserver:~/test$ ls -al
total 8
drwxr-xr-x  2 jk jk 4096 Sep 18 08:22 .
drwxr-xr-x 23 jk jk 4096 Sep 18 08:15 ..
```

8. Text Processing

Linux works with text files in most cases. For example, the configuration files that are stored in /etc are stored as text files. Linux offers a rich set of text processing commands that are quite comprehensive and also time-saving. Knowing their existence and usage helps to avoid the need for writing yet another script (which takes time and effort). In this chapter, we will have a look at these commands and show how to use them.

8.1 Text Processing Commands

cat

Short for concatenate, *cat* outputs the contents of a file to the screen or standard output. The command *cat /etc/passwd* will output all the lines of the file /etc/passwd to the screen.

cat can also write to a text file using the redirect operator ">". To do this, simply use the redirect operator and the name of your text file. For example:

```
cat > output.txt
```

Follow this by the lines of text you wish to output. To quit, press *Ctrl+D*, and type *cat output.txt* to see the result.

Other useful options for *cat* are:

- -E (short for --show-ends): outputs a $ at the end of each line.

- -n (short for --number): numbers all output lines.

- -s (short for --squeeze-blank): suppresses repeated empty output lines.

The *cat* command can also output multiple files at once. The command *cat /etc/passwd /etc/group* will output the contents of /etc/passwd and /etc/group. Keep in mind that the original files are not affected. The next example below outputs the content of the file "output.txt" twice and continuously numbers all the output lines using the option *-n*.

```
user@debian95:~$ cat -n output.txt output.txt
     1  hello world
     2  this is a test
     3  to see if cat works
     4  hello world
     5  this is a test
     6  to see if cat works
user@debian95:~$
```

For a longer example, we are going to create three text files named "file1", "file2" and "file3". Use the commands *cat > file1, cat > file2* and *cat > file3* to create the files. Do not forget to press *Ctrl+D* to exit and use the command *cat file1 file2 file3* to see them all at once.

```
user@debian95:~$ cat > file1
this is file one
user@debian95:~$ cat > file2
this is file two
user@debian95:~$ cat > file3
this is file three
user@debian95:~$ cat file1 file2 file3
this is file one
this is file two
this is file three
user@debian95:~$
```

Using the redirect operator we can then write all three files to one big file.

```
user@debian95:~$ cat file1 file2 file3 > bigfile
user@debian95:~$ cat bigfile
this is file one
this is file two
this is file three
user@debian95:~$
```

tac

The *tac* command works in the same manner as the *cat* command but displays the lines in reverse order. Using "bigfile" from the previous section, let's display the file using *tac*:

```
user@debian95: ~
File  Edit  View  Search  Terminal  Help
user@debian95:~$ tac bigfile
this is file three
this is file two
this is file one
user@debian95:~$
```

more

While *cat* and *tac* display the entire file at once, *more* lets you view the file one screen at a time. Let's say we have a large text file named "alice.txt". To view it type the following:

```
$ more alice.txt
```

This shows a "screenful" of text starting at the beginning of the file. Use the spacebar to scroll through the pages. Alternatively, hitting *enter* scrolls down one line at a time. The disadvantage of the *more* command is that it can only scroll down but not back up again. For that, there is the *less* command.

```
Chapter One - Down the Rabbit Hole: Alice a girl of seven years, is
feeling bored and drowsy while sitting on the riverbank with her
elder sister. She then notices a talking, clothed White Rabbit with
a pocket watch run past. She follows it down a rabbit hole when
suddenly she falls a long way to a curious hall with many locked
doors of all sizes. She finds a small key to a door too small for
her to fit through, but through it she sees an attractive garden.
She then discovers a bottle on a table labelled "DRINK ME", the
contents of which cause her to shrink too small to reach the key
which she has left on the table. She eats a cake with "EAT ME"
written on it in currents as the chapter closes.

Chapter Two - The Pool of Tears: Chapter Two opens with Alice
growing to such a tremendous size her head hits the ceiling. Alice
is unhappy and, as she cries, her tears flood the hallway. After
shrinking down again due to a fan she had picked up, Alice swims
through her own tears and meets a Mouse, who is swimming as well.
She tries to make small talk with him in elementary French
(thinking he may be a French mouse) but her opening gambit "Ou est
ma chatte?" ("Where is my cat?") offends the mouse and he tries to
escape her.
--More--(29%)
```

less

The *less* command is a terminal pager which displays one "screenful" of text at a time and allows scrolling forwards and backward in a file, but it cannot edit a file. Inside *less* there are commands to traverse the file and to find certain patterns:

- j — go down one line.
- k — go up one line.
- g or < — go to the first line.
- G or > — go to the last line.
- <n>G — go to line <n>.
- Space — go to the next page.
- d — go forward half a page.
- b — go to the previous page.
- u — go back half a page.
- v — open page in the editor set by the VISUAL environment variable.
- /<regex> — search forward for <regex>.
- ?<regex> — Search backward for <regex>.
- n — next instance of text matching <regex>.
- N — previous instance of matching <regex>.
- :n — next file when multiple files are opened in the same command.
- :p — previous file when multiple files are opened in the same command.
- q — quit.

head

This command outputs the first *n*-number of lines of a file. If *n* is not specified, it defaults to ten. The image below shows the default use of *head* for the file /etc/ passwd.

To output the first six lines of the file /etc/passwd, type this instead:

```
$ head -n6 /etc/passwd
...
$
```

The opposite of *head* is *tail* which we will explain next.

tail

The *tail* command outputs the last *n*-number of lines of a file. If *n* is not specified, it defaults to ten lines. The image below displays the last 5 lines of the file /etc/passwd.

In addition, *tail* can be used to follow the progress of a log file by using *-f* (or --follow).

As more data gets appended to the end of the file, the output on the screen updates. In order to output the progress of the last 20 lines of /var/log/syslog as it updates, use the following command:

```
$ tail -f -n 20 /var/log/syslog
```

sort

As the name implies, this command is used to sort files. Among others it has the following options:

- -R: random sort.
- -r: reverse the sort order.
- -n: sort numerically.

To sort the first five lines of the file /etc/passwd in alphabetical order, use this command:

```
$ head -n5 /etc/passwd | sort
bin:x:2:2:bin:/bin:/usr/sbin/nologin
daemon:x:1:1:daemon:/usr/sbin:/usr/sbin/nologin
root:x:0:0:root:/root:/bin/bash
sync:x:4:65534:sync:/bin:/bin/sync
sys:x:3:3:sys:/dev:/usr/sbin/nologin
$
```

Use the option *-r* to reverse the sort order:

```
$ head -n5 /etc/passwd | sort -r
sys:x:3:3:sys:/dev:/usr/sbin/nologin
sync:x:4:65534:sync:/bin:/bin/sync
root:x:0:0:root:/root:/bin/bash
daemon:x:1:1:daemon:/usr/sbin:/usr/sbin/nologin
bin:x:2:2:bin:/bin:/usr/sbin/nologin
$
```

uniq

This command reports or removes duplicate lines from a sorted file. Among others it has the following options:

- -c (short for --count): outputs the frequency of occurrence for each line
- -d (short for --repeated): reports the lines that occur more than once, only
- -u (short for --unique): reports the lines that appear only once

The image below shows the basic usage of *uniq*. The output contains each line that only occurs once.

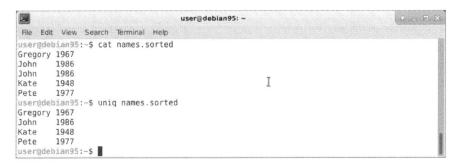

cut

The *cut* command extracts specified fields from files. It requires a delimiter in order to detect the field boundaries. The following example displays the name and the user ID from the file /etc/passwd. These are the first and third fields from each line (option -*f*), and the fields are separated by a ":" (option -*d*).

```
$ cut -d":" -f1,3 /etc/passwd
...
colord:108
saned:109
usbmux:110
geoclue:111
sshd:112
uuidd:113
pulse:114
rtkit:115
avahi:116
...
$
```

grep

This command abbreviates the description "global regular expression print". The command acts as a filter that only prints the lines of text that match a given pattern. *grep* needs data to work on, in combination with a pattern to look for.

Consider the following extract from a file named "places":

```
Amsterdam
Berlin
New York
Bern
Paris
Austin
Cape Town
Tokyo
```

Based on this list, the following command only outputs the lines that contain the character string "Ber". Keep in mind that *grep* is case-sensitive. It does not matter whether the pattern is at the beginning, in the middle or at the end of the text.

```
$ grep Ber places
Berlin
Bern
$
```

grep also supports character strings and regular expressions (RegEx). In order to find all the strings that end with the letter "n" use the option *-E* (or --extended-regexp) followed by the pattern "n$" as shown below:

```
$ grep -E "n$" places
Berlin
Bern
Austin
Cape Town
$
```

tr

The idea behind this command is to translate, to substitute and to delete characters from a string. *tr* reads from "stdin" and outputs to "stdout". It has the following options:

- -d (short for --delete): deletes the given characters from the string
- -s (short for --squeeze-repeats): replaces repeated characters with a single occurrence
- -t (short for --truncate-set1): truncates the given set of characters

The first example shown below demonstrates how to convert lower case to upper case characters. *tr* accepts two sets of characters, the originals, and the replacements. The number of characters in both sets must be the same.

```
user@debian95:~$ cat bigfile
this is file one
this is file two
this is file three
user@debian95:~$ cat bigfile | tr [a-z] [A-Z]
THIS IS FILE ONE
THIS IS FILE TWO
THIS IS FILE THREE
user@debian95:~$
```

The second example demonstrates how to replace repeated spaces with a single one. "space" is defined as a group of characters, being spaces, tabulators, carriage return as well as linefeed.

diff

This tool analyzes two files and prints the lines that are different. Moreover, *diff* outputs a description of which steps are needed to transform the first file into the second one. The image below demonstrates this for two files. The first output line (1c1) means that the first line of file one has to be changed (c for change) in order to get file two. Below that is the referring line from the two files separated by dashes.

```
user@debian95:~$ cat file1
this is file one
with a second line
user@debian95:~$ cat file2
this is file two
with a second line
user@debian95:~$ diff file1 file2
1c1
< this is file one
---
> this is file two
user@debian95:~$
```

93

8.2 Combining Commands

Linux commands on their own are already quite powerful, but you can boost their functionality even further by combining them using a pipe, or redirecting the input/output. We will demonstrate how to achieve this below:

Piping

Piping is a way of connecting two or more commands in a chain. The output of one command is not sent to "stdout" but directly given as an input to the next command. This direct connection between commands allows them to operate simultaneously and permits data to be transferred directly between them continuously, rather than having to pass it through temporary text files or through the display screen. Pipes are unidirectional, in other words, data flows from left to right through the pipeline. The example illustrated below shows the two commands *cat* and *wc* being used to count the number of words in a file.

Redirection

Redirection is a feature in Linux that, when executing a command, can change the standard input/output devices. The basic workflow of any Linux command is that it takes an input and gives an output. The standard input (stdin) device is the keyboard, and the standard output (stdout) device is the screen. With redirection, the standard input/output can be changed. You can read the processed data from a different input source, and output the result to a different place. Output redirection is indicated by the ">" and ">>" symbols, and input redirection by the "<" symbol:

- The > symbol sends the output to the given file and creates a new one. If the file already exists it will be entirely replaced.

- The >> symbol sends the output to the given file and appends it at the end.

- The < symbol reads from the given input source.

The first example below uses the ">>" operator and adds a third line of text at the end of an existing file.

```
user@debian95:~$ echo "line 3" >> file2
user@debian95:~$ cat file2
this is file two
with a second line
line 3
user@debian95:~$
```

The second example goes one step further by redirecting the standard output to a device. The *cat* command reads the file "music.mp3" and sends the output to the device /dev/audio which is the audio device. If the sound configuration in your computer is correct, this command will play the music file.

```
$ cat music.mp3 > /dev/audio
```

The next example combines input and output redirection. The *wc* command reads the content from "file2" and counts the words using the option -*w*. The output is then sent to "stdout" and appended as a new line using the ">>" operator to the file "statistics".

```
user@debian95:~$ cat file2
this is file two
with a second line
line 3
user@debian95:~$
user@debian95:~$ wc -w < file2
10
user@debian95:~$ wc -w < file2 >> statistics
user@debian95:~$ cat statistics
10
user@debian95:~$
```

9. Package Management

In today's world, software can be quite complex. Part of this complexity stems from programs being split into single components made available as single packages, such as binary data, shared libraries and documentation. This concept of software development is called "modularity", and is generally accepted and in widespread use. Debian, for instance, offers more than 60,000 different packages.

Package management covers all actions needed to handle these software packages including installation, configuration, removal, and updating packages. It also covers resolving package dependencies (packages that depend on each other).

9.1 Understanding Package Architecture

To explain the Linux package architecture, we will be using Debian for illustration. The Debian distribution is known for its stability and exceptional packaging system. The descriptions that follow are valid for all Linux distributions that are derived from Debian, such as Ubuntu, Linux Mint, Knoppix, Kali Linux, Grml and Xandros. Keep in mind that the names of packages may differ, as well as the distribution-specific package mirrors and the names of package classes.

The Debian package management ecosystem contains quite a number of different components such as package lists, package sources and package mirrors, different software packages, software to manage the package setup, and the package cache. These components are explained in more detail below.

Package Lists

Debian contains a list of available software packages. This list is referenced in the file /etc/apt/sources, and for specific components and personal additions in the files in the directory /etc/apt/sources.list.d. As an example, the messenger "Skype" uses the file "skype-stable.list". The lists use a text format with one package source per line:

deb http://ftp.de.debian.org/debian/ stretch main contrib non-free deb-src http://ftp.de.debian.org/debian/ stretch main contrib non-free

Each line either refers to a binary package type (deb) or to a source package type (deb-src). The package type is followed by the package source, which refers to a repository that provides the software packages. Next, the line contains the name of the Debian release, which can be specified either as the nickname of the release or the branch.

The nickname originates from a character of the film "Toy Story". The branch refers to the development stage of the release, and can be oldoldstable (pre-previous release), oldstable (previous release), stable (current release), testing (next release), unstable (future release) or experimental. After the name of the branch, the package classes are named.

The entries for security updates of Debian 9 Stretch look as follows:

```
deb http://security.debian.org/ stretch/updates main contrib non-free
deb-src http://security.debian.org/ stretch/updates main contrib non-free
```

In order to refresh the package list from the referenced package sources, invoke the following command:

```
# apt-get update
```

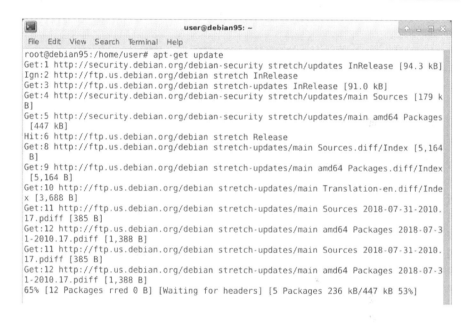

Package Sources

The Debian project maintains an official list of package sources named "package mirrors". This list is divided into primary and secondary package mirrors. Primary package mirrors offer the full spectrum of supported architectures, while secondary mirrors only offer a subset.

For the United States, the official primary package mirror is:

```
ftp.us.debian.org
```

You can view the current state of your desired package mirror here:

Package Types

Debian divides its packages into three categories:

- Main - free packages.
- Contrib - free packages that depend on non-free packages.
- Non-free - non-free packages that do not provide source code.

Packages that belong to the non-free category include firmware drivers, Skype messenger, and the Flash plugin. Every single entry in the list of source packages specifies their category of software.

Package Management Tools

In order to maintain the selection of software packages installed on your Linux system, a number of tools are available:

- dpkg - used to manage single packages.
- apt, aptitude, synaptic - used to manage packages with their dependencies.
- tasksel - used to manage entire software collections (tasks).

The image below depicts the different levels on which the tools operate and how they work together. The two boxes with dotted outlines refer to the shared libraries that handle the package management tasks.

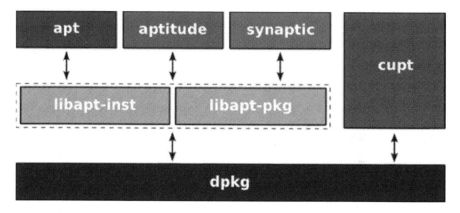

On the lower level, we have "dpkg". Its task is to install a single Debian package or to remove the contents of a package that has already been installed. In order to query packages and files, it makes use of the two tools "dpkg-deb" and "dpkg-query". "dpkg" allows you to maintain your package base but does not handle package dependencies.

Typically, the upper level is represented by the tools "apt", "aptitude" and "synaptic". These tools have the task of simplifying package management by combining all actions into one application. These tools use either the shared libraries "libapt-inst" or "libapt-pkg", or communicate with "dpkg" to perform the package management tasks. This includes handling the package dependencies.

Package Cache

The package cache is located at /var/cache/apt/archives. Whenever you install a software package via "apt-get" or "aptitude" the appropriate package is retrieved and stored locally at this path. To illustrate, below lists the cached "deb" packages using *ls*.

```
$ ls /var/cache/apt/archives/*.deb
/var/cache/apt/archives/cpuid_20140123-2_amd64.deb
/var/cache/apt/archives/libxml2-utils_2.9.1+dfsg1-5+deb8u7_amd64.deb
/var/cache/apt/archives/python3-bitarray_0.8.1-1_amd64.deb
/var/cache/apt/archives/python-bitarray_0.8.1-1_amd64.deb
$
```

The more software you install, the more "deb" packages are cached. It is recommended to clear the package cache from time to time by using either *aptitude* or *apt-cache*:

```
# aptitude clean
```

```
# apt-cache clean
```

9.2 Day-to-Day Administration Tasks

This section deals with basic package management actions needed in day-to-day life as a system administrator.

Displaying Installed Packages

The command *dpkg -l* lists the installed packages and their status. The image below shows the output.

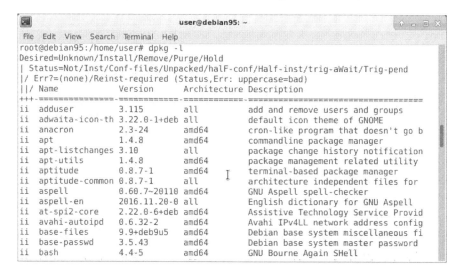

The single columns contain the following information:

- status - the status of the package, such as fully installed (ii) or removed and still configured (rc).
- name - the name of the package.
- version - the package version.
- architecture - the architecture or platform the package is built for.
- description - a short description of the package

Installing a Package

In order to install a package, use the *apt-get* command. The output below shows this for the "htop" package.

```
user@debian95: ~
File  Edit  View  Search  Terminal  Help
root@debian95:/home/user# apt-get install htop
Reading package lists... Done
Building dependency tree
Reading state information... Done
Suggested packages:
  strace
The following NEW packages will be installed:
  htop
0 upgraded, 1 newly installed, 0 to remove and 35 not upgraded.
Need to get 88.2 kB of archives.
After this operation, 224 kB of additional disk space will be used.
Get:1 http://ftp.us.debian.org/debian stretch/main amd64 htop amd64 2.0.2-1 [88.2 kB
]
Fetched 88.2 kB in 1s (76.6 kB/s)
Selecting previously unselected package htop.
(Reading database ... 82741 files and directories currently installed.)
Preparing to unpack .../htop_2.0.2-1_amd64.deb ...
Unpacking htop (2.0.2-1) ...
Processing triggers for mime-support (3.60) ...
Processing triggers for desktop-file-utils (0.23-1) ...
Processing triggers for man-db (2.7.6.1-2) ...
Setting up htop (2.0.2-1) ...
root@debian95:/home/user#
```

Updating an Installed Package

Updating an installed package is quite easy and done in the following way. First, update the package list using *apt-get update* as described earlier in this chapter. Then run *apt-get install* to update the package. If an updated version of the package is available, the new package will be retrieved from the package mirror, the old package will be removed, and the new one will be installed.

Removing an Installed Package

Removing an installed package is done in a similar way as installing or updating. The *apt-get* command has the option to remove the package as shown below.

```
root@debian95:/home/user# apt-get remove htop
Reading package lists... Done
Building dependency tree
Reading state information... Done
The following packages will be REMOVED:
  htop
0 upgraded, 0 newly installed, 1 to remove and 35 not upgraded.
After this operation, 224 kB disk space will be freed.
Do you want to continue? [Y/n]
(Reading database ... 82751 files and directories currently installed.)
Removing htop (2.0.2-1) ...
Processing triggers for mime-support (3.60) ...
Processing triggers for desktop-file-utils (0.23-1) ...
Processing triggers for man-db (2.7.6.1-2) ...
root@debian95:/home/user#
```

This step removes all of the package content except for the configuration files. In order to entirely remove the package with its configuration files, add the switch *--purge* as follows:

```
# apt-get remove --purge htop
...
#
```

10. Log Files

There are moments in Linux administration when you will have to figure out why your system behaves in a rather unexpected way. This is where log files come into play. These kinds of files record the behavior of the system and help you to find out what happened at any point in time. The log files are stored in the directory /var/log. Which log files are important for you will depend on your system and your requirements.

10.1 Important Log Files

The log files explained below are, among others, the most important in server systems.

/var/log/messages

This is the most important log file in Linux. It persistently records generic system events, such as system error messages, system startups and shutdowns, as well as changes in the network configuration. The example below contains the log messages that are recorded as soon as a phone (USB device) is connected:

Oct	4 15:10:37 debian95 kernel: [532994.056321] usb 2-2: USB disconnect, device number - 16

Oct	4 15:10:37 debian95 kernel: [532994.391279] usb 2-2: new high-speed USB device - number 17 using xhci_hcd
Oct	4 15:10:37 debian95 kernel: [532994.520991] usb 2-2: New USB device found, - idVendor=04e8, idProduct=6860
Oct	4 15:10:37 debian95 kernel: [532994.520993] usb 2-2: New USB device strings: Mfr - =1, Product=2, SerialNumber=3
Oct	4 15:10:37 debian95 kernel: [532994.520994] usb 2-2: Product: SAMSUNG_Android
Oct	4 15:10:37 debian95 kernel: [532994.520995] usb 2-2: Manufacturer: SAMSUNG
...	

/var/log/lastlog

This file records which user logged into the Linux system. Use the *lastlog* command to see the login statistics. We'll discuss this command in more detail in a later chapter.

/var/log/auth.log

All authentication-related events in Debian and Ubuntu servers are logged here. If you are looking for anything involving the user authorization mechanism, you can find it in this log file.

/var/log/kern.log

Here you will find messages that relate to the Linux kernel.

```
...
Oct    8 19:19:34 debian95 kernel: [893330.867019] usb 2-1:
       new low-speed USB device -
       number 37 using xhci_hcd
Oct    8 19:19:34 debian95 kernel: [893331.000139] usb 2-1:
       New USB device found, -
       idVendor=046d, idProduct=c03d
Oct    8 19:19:34 debian95 kernel: [893331.000142] usb 2-1:
       New USB device strings: Mfr -
       =1, Product=2, SerialNumber=0
Oct    8 19:19:34 debian95 kernel: [893331.000144] usb 2-1:
       Product: USB-PS/2 Optical -
       Mouse
Oct    8 19:19:34 debian95 kernel: [893331.000145] usb 2-1:
       Manufacturer: Logitech
Oct    8 19:19:34 debian95 kernel: [893331.000259] usb 2-1: ep
       0x81 - rounding interval -
       to 64 microframes, ep desc says 80 microframes
...
```

/var/log/dpkg.log

This file belongs to "dpkg" (which we discussed in the previous chapter) and records the changes relating to installed, updated and removed packages.

```
...
2018-10-06 21:52:41 startup packages configure
2018-10-06 21:53:21 startup archives unpack
2018-10-06 21:53:21 upgrade php5-gd:amd64 5.6.36+dfsg-
       0+deb8u1 5.6.38+dfsg-0+deb8u1
2018-10-06 21:53:21 status triggers-pending libapache2-mod-
       php5:amd64 5.6.36+dfsg-0+ -
       deb8u1
```

```
2018-10-06 21:53:21 status half-configured php5-gd:amd64
    5.6.36+dfsg-0+deb8u1
2018-10-06 21:53:21 status unpacked php5-gd:amd64 5.6.36+dfsg-
    0+deb8u1
2018-10-06 21:53:21 status half-installed php5-gd:amd64
    5.6.36+dfsg-0+deb8u1
2018-10-06 21:53:21 status half-installed php5-gd:amd64
    5.6.36+dfsg-0+deb8u1
...
```

/var/log/apt/history

Similar to the previous file, this file records the changes made by "apt" relating to installed, updated and removed packages.

```
....
Start-Date: 2018-10-06 21:50:02
Upgrade: imagemagick-6.q16:amd64 (6.8.9.9-5+deb8u13, 6.8.9.9-
    5+deb8u14), imagemagick: -
    amd64 (6.8.9.9-5+deb8u13, 6.8.9.9-5+deb8u14)
End-Date: 2018-10-06 21:50:04

Start-Date: 2018-10-06 21:51:05
Upgrade: bind9-host:amd64 (9.9.5.dfsg-9+deb8u15, 9.9.5.dfsg-
    9+deb8u16), liblwres90: -
    amd64 (9.9.5.dfsg-9+deb8u15, 9.9.5.dfsg-9+deb8u16),
    libdns100:amd64 (9.9.5.dfsg-9+ -
    deb8u15, 9.9.5.dfsg-9+deb8u16), libisccfg90:amd64
    (9.9.5.dfsg-9+deb8u15, 9.9.5.dfsg -
    -9+deb8u16), libbind9-90:amd64 (9.9.5.dfsg-9+deb8u15,
    9.9.5.dfsg-9+deb8u16), -
    dnsutils:amd64 (9.9.5.dfsg-9+deb8u15, 9.9.5.dfsg-
    9+deb8u16), libisc95:amd64 (9.9.5. -
    dfsg-9+deb8u15, 9.9.5.dfsg-9+deb8u16)
End-Date: 2018-10-06 21:51:07
....
```

10.2 Essential Commands & Graphical Tools

In addition to the log files covered above, there are system commands available to display relevant information for your machine.

dmesg

As covered at the beginning of this guide, this command allows you to view the entire boot process including BIOS messages.

```
# dmesg
```

journalctl -b

Also covered in Chapter 1, this command shows the boot messages of your system.

```
# journalctl -b
```

journalctl _UID=1000

This command shows the log entries for a specific user. In this instance, it shows the entries for the user with the User ID "1000".

```
# journalctl _UID=1000
```

111

journalctl --disk-usage

In order to see how much disk space is needed to store the log files, use the switch *--disk-usage* as follows:

For system administrators, it is quite common to use command line tools like *tail*, *cat* or *grep*. But if you prefer graphical tools, two great options to consider are the log file navigators "lnav" or "glogg". Both are shown below.

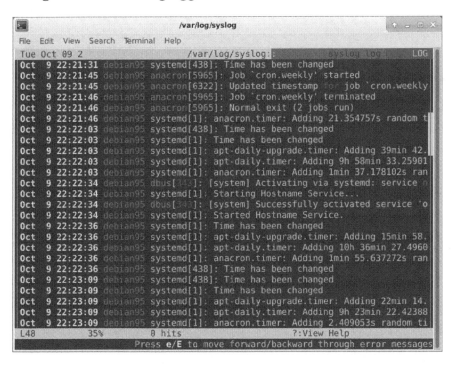

11. Process Management

Understanding the execution of a program is essential for being a good system administrator. In this chapter, we will be looking at processes in greater detail, as well as how to work with and manipulate processes. A running instance of a program is known as a process. It is made up of the program instruction, data read from files, as well as other programs or inputs from a system user.

Every process is assigned a Process ID (PID) which allows the system to keep track of all processes. The system boot process has a PID 0, then the initial process has a PID 1, and so on in a sequential manner. The initial process PID 1 refers to /sbin/initd on older Linux systems or /sbin/systemd on contemporary Linux systems.

11.1 Working with Processes

ps and pstree

In order to list all the running processes, use either the *ps* command or the *pstree* command.

The output of *ps* as shown above consists of four columns that have the following meanings:

- PID - the process ID.
- TTY - the terminal from which the command was invoked.
- TIME - the time the process has been active.
- CMD - the command that was invoked.

The following switches can be used to retrieve additional information regarding the processes:

- -e and ax: show all processes.
- -p: shows information for the given process id only.

```
$ ps -p 26426
PID     TTY     STAT    TIME    COMMAND
26426   pts/9   Ss      0:00    bash
$
```

- -C: shows processes that refer to the given command name.

```
$ ps -C bash
PID     TTY     TIME        CMD
1808    pts/0   00:00:00    bash
4537    pts/4   00:00:00    bash
4760    pts/5   00:00:00    bash
5281    pts/1   00:00:00    bash
8213    pts/2   00:00:03    bash
15880   pts/12  00:00:00    bash
20724   pts/3   00:00:00    bash
20935   pts/7   00:00:00    bash
$
```

- -u: shows processes that belong to the given username.

```
$ ps -u fritz
PID    TTY      TIME        CMD
1341   ?        00:00:00    systemd
1406.  ?        00:00:32    xfwm4
1408   ?        00:01:10    xfce4-panel
1410   ?        00:00:15    xfdesktop
1411   ?        00:00:05    xfsettingsd
1413   ?        00:00:05    x-www-browser
1415   ?        00:00:06    xfce4-power-man
1418   ?        00:00:00    gvfsd
1808   pts/0    00:00:00    bash
1841   pts/0    1-06:21:26  iceweasel
4537   pts/4    00:00:00    bash
4760   pts/5    00:00:00    bash
5281   pts/1    00:00:00    bash
$
```

The *pstree* command is similar to the *ps* command but displays the processes as a hierarchical tree. A useful switch is *-p* which adds the process ID to the process name.

```
root@debian95:/home/user# pstree
systemd─┬─agetty
        ├─cron
        ├─dbus-daemon
        ├─dhclient
        ├─polkitd───┬─{gdbus}
        │           └─{gmain}
        ├─pulseaudio─┬─{alsa-sink-Intel}
        │            └─{alsa-source-Int}
        ├─rsyslogd─┬─{in:imklog}
        │          ├─{in:imuxsock}
        │          └─{rs:main Q:Reg}
        ├─rtkit-daemon───2*[{rtkit-daemon}]
        ├─sshd
        ├─systemd─┬─(sd-pam)
        │         ├─at-spi-bus-laun─┬─dbus-daemon
        │         │                 ├─{dconf worker}
        │         │                 ├─{gdbus}
        │         │                 └─{gmain}
        │         ├─at-spi2-registr─┬─{gdbus}
        │         │                 └─{gmain}
        │         ├─dbus-daemon
        │         ├─dconf-service─┬─{gdbus}
        │         │               └─{gmain}
```

pidof

The *pidof* command simply displays the ID of the specified process. The image below returns the PID of the processes that run "bash".

pgrep

This command searches the list of processes for the specified process name. The image below displays the processes that match the string "xfce".

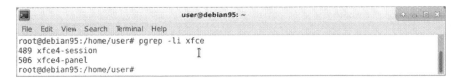

top

The *top* command displays the processes according to their activity. The most active process is on top, followed by the less active ones. The list is updated every second. The single columns contain the process ID (titled PID), the user name of the owner of the process (titled USER), the process priority (titled PR), the nice level (titled NI), the virtual memory usage (titled VIRT), the reserved memory (titled RES), the shared memory (titled SHR), both the percentile CPU and memory usage (titled %CPU and %MEM), the running time of the process (titled TIME+) as well as the command that was used to invoke the process (titled COMMAND).

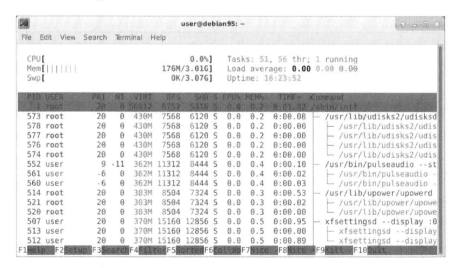

htop

"htop" is an additional software package and contains a more interactive version of *top*. The arrangement of the columns is similar to *top*.

Foreground and Background Processes

There are two types of processes: foreground and background processes.

Foreground processes are initialized and controlled through a terminal session. In other words, there has to be a user connected to the system to start these processes and the process occupies the terminal while it is executing. In contrast, background processes are not connected to the terminal and do not explicitly require any user input. They hence do not occupy the terminal while waiting to be completed and allow you to run multiple processes.

Processes can be initialized in the background with the use of the "&" symbol.

```
$ process1 &
...
$
```

To send a running process to the background, use the command *bg* followed by the job ID, while *fg* will send the process to the foreground. You can use the *jobs* command to show the jobs that are currently running and their associated job IDs:

```
$ process1 &
$ process2 &
$ jobs
[1]+ Running process1
[2]- Running process2
$
```

Stopping and Terminating Processes

In the event that a running program becomes unresponsive and causes load, what can we do to stop it and get rid of it? Luckily we have a few options that allow us to send a specific signal to the program in order to stop it.

The command used in this instance is the *kill* command with a corresponding switch. Among others, these signals exist:

- SIGHUP (1) - Hang up signal. Programs can listen for this signal and act upon it. This signal is sent to processes running in a terminal when you close the terminal.

- SIGINT (2) - Interrupt signal. This signal is given to processes to interrupt them. Programs can process this signal and act upon it. You can also issue this signal directly by typing CTRL+C in the terminal window where the program is running.

- SIGTERM (15) - Termination signal. This signal is given to processes to terminate them. Again, programs can process this signal and act upon it, for example writing data to a file before terminating. This is the default signal sent by the *kill* command if no signal is specified.

- SIGKILL (9) - Kill signal. This signal causes the immediate termination of the process by the Linux kernel. Programs cannot listen for this signal.

In order to terminate and kill a program named "hangingProgram" you will have to identify the program first. You do this by using *pgrep* to find the associated process as follows:

```
$ pgrep hangingProgram
3167
$
```

Next, send the identified process the *SIGTERM* signal:

```
$ kill -SIGTERM 3167
```

As an alternative, you may invoke *kill* as follows:

```
$ kill -15 3167
```

Or you may stop the hanging process by pressing CTRL+Z, and then deleting the process using this command:

```
$ kill -SIGKILL 3167
```

As demonstrated above, this command does the same:

```
$ kill -9 3167
```

Adjusting the Execution Priority of a Process

The processors of your machine can manage more than one task at the same time. We can set guidelines for the CPU to follow when it's looking at the different tasks it has to execute. These guidelines are called "niceness" or "nice values". The Linux niceness scale goes from -20 to 19, where a lower number represents a higher priority for a task. If the niceness value is high like 19, the task will be set to the lowest priority and the CPU will process it whenever it gets a chance. The default nice value is zero.

You can display the nice level of a process using *ps* as follows:

```
$ ps -o pid,comm,nice -p 1808
PID COMMAND NI
1808 bash 0
$
```

The first column contains the Process ID (PID), the second column contains the command, and the third contains the nice level (NI). As demonstrated in the example above, the "bash" process with the PID 1808 has a nice level of 0.

An existing process' nice level can be adjusted using the *renice* command. In order to reduce the nice level of the process above to 10, issue the command below. Keep in mind that only root can apply negative nice values to a process.

```
$ renice 10 -p 1808
```

12. System and Network Security

The idea behind this chapter is to develop a basic understanding of how to set up and run a secure system. In the following section, we focus on a more practical approach and will have a look at the detection of open ports, existing and active users, limiting remote access, updating software, and making use of the computing power made available.

12.1 Open Ports

If you've been following along since our beginner's guide, you might recall that we set up our Linux distribution with a minimalistic installation. We installed only the software packages that we actually needed, and post-installed other software if it was necessary later on. We recommend this for all new installations, as the result is a very lean system with high performance that requires as little resources as possible. The second reason is the limited software restricts the number of potential security issues from inside the system.

As the next step, we will check the number of services that are available from outside the Linux system. This is known as port scanning.

The tools that will assist us are the command line tools "netcat" and "nmap" (short for Network Mapper) as well as its graphical pendant "zenmap".

netcat

The following *netcat* command starts scanning the local desktop system (localhost) for available network services on ports between 1 and 1024. The switch *-zv* enables verbose scanning of ports:

```
$ nc -zv localhost 1-1024
localhost [127.0.0.1] 631 (ipp) open
localhost [127.0.0.1] 111 (sunrpc) open
localhost [127.0.0.1] 80 (http) open
localhost [127.0.0.1] 25 (smtp) open
localhost [127.0.0.1] 22 (ssh) open
$
```

netcat reports one detected service per line. The results from the example above are the Internet Printing Protocol (IPP) on port 631, Sunrpc services on port 111, Hypertext Transfer Protocol (HTTP) on port 80, Simple Message Transfer Protocol (SMTP) on port 25, and Secure Shell (SSH) on port 22.

Detecting the open ports on our example Linux server gives us a slightly different picture. The image below shows the result of our scanning. As you can see *netcat* accepts various inputs: a single port, an entire port range, or the service name. If the service is available it returns "open", otherwise it returns "connection refused".

```
user@debian95:~$ nc -zv localhost 1-1024
localhost [127.0.0.1] 22 (ssh) open
user@debian95:~$ nc -zv localhost ssh
localhost [127.0.0.1] 22 (ssh) open
user@debian95:~$ nc -zv localhost ftp
localhost [127.0.0.1] 21 (ftp) : Connection refused
user@debian95:~$ nc -zv localhost http
localhost [127.0.0.1] 80 (http) : Connection refused
user@debian95:~$
```

nmap and zenmap

The next command we will look at is *nmap*. The switch *-T4* sets the timing and *-A* enables the detection of the operating system. This step is called OS probing. The following call does this for the local system:

```
$ nmap -T4 -A localhost
```

The report is quite detailed and contains information about the detected operating system as well as the services.

```
user@debian95:~$ nmap -T4 -A localhost

Starting Nmap 7.40 ( https://nmap.org ) at 2018-10-05 10:39 CEST
Nmap scan report for localhost (127.0.0.1)
Host is up (0.00013s latency).
Other addresses for localhost (not scanned): ::1
Not shown: 999 closed ports
PORT    STATE SERVICE VERSION
22/tcp open  ssh     OpenSSH 7.4p1 Debian 10+deb9u3 (protocol 2.0)
| ssh-hostkey:
|   2048 0d:9e:f0:07:f4:86:33:c1:77:24:d6:4b:af:c7:c2:78 (RSA)
|_  256 22:83:b2:bc:b2:7d:64:6b:86:b2:6b:e6:c2:d4:45:6c (ECDSA)
Service Info: OS: Linux; CPE: cpe:/o:linux:linux_kernel

Service detection performed. Please report any incorrect results at https://nmap.org/submi
t/ .
Nmap done: 1 IP address (1 host up) scanned in 0.55 seconds
user@debian95:~$
```

Below we used "zenmap" to scan our Linux system, which provides us with the same result as above. Both results show that the only service that is enabled and accessible from outside, is OpenSSH (short for Open Secure Shell).

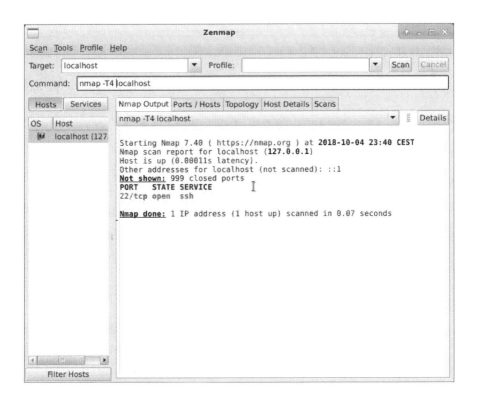

12.2 Local and Remote Users

Security of a Linux system includes the users and their accounts. In our beginner's guide we had a look at basic commands such as *w*, *who* and *users*. Now we will address more sophisticated methods of detecting user information.

To see which local accounts exist, you can have a look at the file /etc/passwd and verify the entries. The user ID of a regular user account starts at 1000.

In order to see which local users logged into the system, the *lslogins* command can be used. *lslogins* extracts the user information from the different configuration files and displays the result in a very nice way. Invoked as a regular user without further switches, *lslogins* displays the user ID, the account name, the number of logins, and the content of the GECOS field.

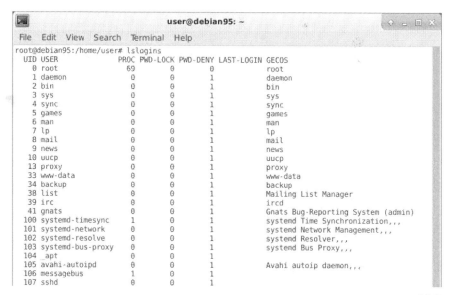

Invoked as an administrative user, *lslogins* adds the information for the two columns PWD-LOCK and PWD-DENY. These columns show if the associated account is locked or if login via password is denied.

In order to see the detailed information for a specific user, *lslogins* utilizes the switches *-u* followed by a username, as well as *-- time iso* to display the time in a readable format.

```
root@debian95:/home/user# lslogins -u user --time iso
Username:                              user
UID:                                   1000
Gecos field:                           Debian User,123,456,135
Home directory:                        /home/user
Shell:                                 /bin/bash
No login:                              no
Password is locked:                    no
Password not required:                 no
Login by password disabled:            no
Primary group:                         user
GID:                                   1000
Supplementary groups:                  bluetooth,cdrom,floppy,audio,dip,video,plugdev,netdev
Supplementary group IDs:               111,24,25,29,30,44,46,108
Hushed:                                no
Password expiration warn interval:     7
Password changed:                      2018-08-20
Maximum change time:                   99999
Running processes:                     32

Last logs:
2018-10-05T12:11:19+0200 systemd[438]: Time has been changed
2018-10-05T12:11:52+0200 systemd[438]: Time has been changed
2018-10-05T12:12:24+0200 systemd[438]: Time has been changed

root@debian95:/home/user#
```

As explained above, *lslogins* evaluates the local login attempts only. To retrieve login attempts from remote systems, use the *getent* command. It also evaluates databases that support the Name Service Switch library (NSS) which is configured in /etc/nsswitch.conf and covers services like Lightweight Directory Access Protocol (LDAP) and Network Information Systems (NIS). In order to get information for user "caro" invoke *getent* as follows:

```
$ getent passwd caro
caro:x:1005:1005:Caro,,,:/home/caro:/bin/bash
$
```

The two commands *last* and *lastlog* can also be used to show which users logged in last. *last* reports a detailed login as shown below. The columns contain the username, the terminal, and the session information.

```
$ last
user     pts/13    :0    Fri Oct 5 09:41 still logged in
user     pts/13    :0    Thu Oct 4 15:12 - 15:24 (00:12)
user     pts/13    :0    Thu Oct 4 14:28 - 14:59 (00:31)
user     pts/11    :0    Thu Oct 4 14:12 still logged in
user     pts/8     :0    Thu Oct 4 14:04 still logged in
user     pts/8     :0    Thu Oct 4 11:34 - 11:49 (00:15)
$
```

The *lastlog* command prints the statistics for which users logged in last. The first image below shows this for all users and the second image for a specific user.

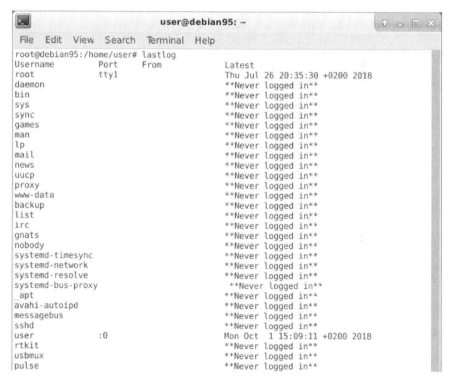

12.3 Restricting Remote Access

Linux has the ability to limit remote access to the system. The two files /etc/hosts.allow and /etc/hosts.deny regulate the access from other systems for TCP-based services. The limitation covers single hosts, IP addresses, and entire network segments.

The file /etc/hosts.allow explicitly allows access, and /etc/hosts.deny forbids access. Because access rules in the file /etc/hosts.allow are applied first, they take precedence over rules specified in /etc/hosts.deny. Therefore, if access to a service is allowed in /etc/hosts.allow, a rule denying access to that same service in /etc/hosts.deny is ignored.

The first example illustrates how to limit access via SSH for all devices that have a hostname ending in "example.net":

```
# /etc/hosts.deny
ALL: ALL
# /etc/hosts.allow
sshd : .example.net
```

The second example limits access for devices that have an IP address from the 192.168.30.* subnet:

```
# /etc/hosts.deny
ALL: ALL
# /etc/hosts.allow
ALL : 192.168.30.*
```

The third example shows how to allow access for all devices that have a hostname ending in "example.net" except "login.example.net":

```
# /etc/hosts.deny
ALL: ALL
# /etc/hosts.allow
sshd : .example.net EXCEPT login.example.net
```

Note that TCP wrapped services do not cache the rules from the host access files, so any changes to /etc/hosts.allow or /etc/hosts.deny will take effect immediately without restarting network services.

12.4 Unused Software

Apart from ports and accounts, we must also have a look at the software that is installed on the system. As we mentioned earlier, when it comes to software: the less the better. The idea behind this rule is to keep your server lean and mean. Install only those packages that you really need. If there are unwanted packages that provide services that are not in use, remove them. The fewer packages installed, the less chance of unpatched code and security issues.

Software packages that are left-overs can be identified using "deborphan". The image below shows that "deborphan" discovered two packages, "iceweasel" and "netcat". The first column displays the package size, followed by the package category (main/oldlibs), the package name, and the package class (extra).

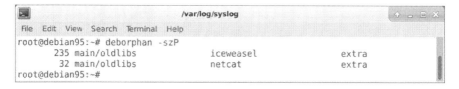

Packages that are no longer needed can be removed using the command below. This cleans the system from unused libraries and old dependencies that are left over.

```
# apt-get autoremove
```

Removing unused software helps a lot. It's also important to keep the remaining packages up-to-date, which we discussed in Chapter 9.

> **How did we do?**
>
> Did we meet your expectations? My wife and I put a lot of effort into this guide, spending many late nights adding examples and tweaking formats, and would love to get your genuine feedback on what you thought about it. Leave us a short review on Amazon and tell us: What were your expectations when you bought this guide? Did we live up to them? What would you change? What other guides would you want to see?
>
>

Further Reading

For further reading on Linux, keep a lookout for more books within this series coming soon.

About the Author

Nathan Clark is an expert programmer with nearly 20 years of experience in the software industry.

With a master's degree from MIT, he has worked for some of the leading software companies in the United States and built up extensive knowledge of software design and development.

Nathan and his wife, Sarah, started their own development firm in 2009 to be able to take on more challenging and creative projects. Today they assist high-caliber clients from all over the world.

Nathan enjoys sharing his programming knowledge through his book series, developing innovative software solutions for their clients and watching classic sci-fi movies in his free time.

Made in the USA
Columbia, SC
22 December 2019